ANDREW JACKSON

PRESIDENTIAL ✧ LEADERS

ANDREW JACKSON

CAROL H. BEHRMAN

LERNER PUBLICATIONS COMPANY / MINNEAPOLIS

To Patrick, Matthew, Luke, Jonathan, and Rose—American heroes of the future

Lerner Publications Company
A division of Lerner Publishing Group
241 First Avenue North
Minneapolis, MN 55401 U.S.A.

Website address: www.lernerbooks.com

Library of Congress Cataloging-in-Publication Data

Behrman, Carol H.
    Andrew Jackson / by Carol H. Behrman.
        p.   cm. — (Presidential leaders)
    Summary: A biography of the seventh president from his childhood in South Carolina, through his military career in the War of 1812 and his family life, to his legacy as America's first populist president.
    Includes bibliographical references and index.
    ISBN: 0-8225-0093-0 (lib. bdg. : alk. paper)
    1. Jackson, Andrew, 1767–1845—Juvenile literature. 2. Presidents—United States—Biography—Juvenile literature. [1. Jackson, Andrew, 1767–1845. 2. Presidents.]
    I. Title. II. Series.
    E382 .B44 2003
    973.5'6'092—dc21   2001008165

Manufactured in the United States of America
1 2 3 4 5 6 – JR – 08 07 06 05 04 03

CONTENTS

Overjoyed by the election of President Andrew Jackson, thousands of Americans streamed into Washington, D.C., to attend the inauguration in March 1829.

INTRODUCTION

"As long as our Government is administered for the good of the people, and is regulated by their will . . . it will be worth defending."
—Andrew Jackson's First Inaugural
Address, 1829

On the afternoon of March 4, 1829, the elegant rooms of the President's House in Washington, D.C., were in chaos. For the first time in history, the general public was invited to a president's inaugural reception—and thousands of people came, cheering and yelling. They stomped in with muddy boots, staining and tearing the beautiful carpets. They guzzled drinks and gobbled cake. Men fought and knocked each other down. Women fainted. Tables were overturned, sending china and glasses crashing to the floor. The president's friends, fearing for his safety, led him out a back door and took him to a nearby hotel.

When the crowd of overenthusiastic guests had gone, the president returned to the scene of the party. It might be a mess, but it was his new home. And many of the people at the party had helped to bring him here. Some of them were common, hardworking folks, struggling pioneers of the American frontier. They loved him as one of their own. Some were soldiers whom he had led into battle. They respected and adored him. They called him Old Hickory.

Not everyone liked him. Powerful people of wealth and property mistrusted him, thinking of him as a wild man from across the mountains. The Native Americans whom he forced out of their homes hated and feared him. Some of his closest friends became his bitterest enemies when they were victims of his quick temper. He was always ready to risk his life and reputation out of loyalty to a person or a cause, but he could quickly turn against someone who insulted him or his honor.

This man, who inspired such deep and different emotions in others, was Andrew Jackson. He was the son of immigrants, the hero of the Battle of New Orleans, and the seventh president of the United States.

CHAPTER ONE

BOYHOOD IN THE WAXHAWS

*"[He] was a wild, frolicsome, willful,
mischievous, daring, reckless boy."*
—James Parton

Andrew's father, also named Andrew Jackson, came to the
American colonies from Castlereagh in northern Ireland in
1765. The thirteen American colonies, stretching from New
Hampshire to Georgia, belonged to England. Their inhabitants were subjects of the British king. Like Andrew Jackson's
family, most settlers were immigrants from the British Isles
hoping to find exciting opportunities and better lives.

The elder Andrew Jackson arrived in this new world
with his lively, red-haired wife, Elizabeth, and their sons,
two-year-old Hugh and five-month-old Robert. Following
the trail of other pioneers before them, they set forth
southwest from Pennsylvania along the Catawba Traders'
Path. They settled in a frontier region called the Waxhaws,

a remote area on the western border of the Carolinas. It
was a dangerous and isolated back country, where disagreements between neighbors were often settled by violence.

By the time the Jacksons arrived in the Waxhaws, the
best land had already been claimed by other settlers.
Andrew, Elizabeth, and their boys had to make do with two
hundred acres in an area along Twelve Mile Creek. The red
soil was thin and barren, dotted with stands of scrubby
pine, hickory, and oak. But Andrew Jackson was determined to make a home for his young family out of their
wilderness acres. He and Elizabeth worked long and hard.
By 1767 they had managed to clear some of the land and
build a log house.

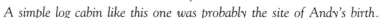

A simple log cabin like this one was probably the site of Andy's birth.

Creating a farm out of this rough country was back-breaking, brutal work. Andrew Jackson's father was only twenty-nine years old when he died after injuring himself trying to move a heavy log. On the day of the funeral, a thick blanket of snow covered the Waxhaws. The grieving Elizabeth was nine months pregnant. She, Hugh, and Robert accompanied a horse-drawn sled that carried the body of their husband and father. They stumbled and slipped over broken ice covering creeks and streams. Finally, they arrived at the small churchyard where other mourners waited, shivering in the cold. There, to everyone's horror, someone discovered that the sled was empty. The coffin had slipped off along the way. Neighbors scurried back to retrieve it from the brush in which it had been caught and brought it to the graveyard. The young immigrant who had dreamed of greatness in a new land was laid to rest under the red earth of the Waxhaws.

A NEW ARRIVAL

On March 15, 1767, Andrew and Elizabeth's third son was born and named after his father. No one but the Jacksons and their relatives bothered to note this birth, and no one is even certain whether the portion of the Waxhaws where baby Andy Jackson came into the world is in present-day North or South Carolina.

Elizabeth Jackson and her three sons moved in with her sister, Jane Crawford, and Jane's husband and children. Frontier life was tough and grueling, and any extra pair of hands was welcome to share the work. When the boys were old enough, they helped their uncle with the farm and the livestock. Aunt Jane was sickly, so Elizabeth took over most of the never-ending household chores herself. When Jane died, Elizabeth managed the household alone, looking after the Crawfords' eight youngsters in addition to her own three boys.

A FRONTIER SPIRIT

Andy Jackson's humble boyhood was no different from that of other frontier youngsters of the time. In some ways, Andy's life was even harder than most. He never had a father to support his family or to guide his steps. But Andy was tough. As the years passed, he grew into a tall, strong boy. He worked hard at his chores on the Crawford farm and didn't complain.

School was a different story. Andy's mother hoped that her youngest son might become a minister. Elizabeth Jackson was deeply religious. She taught her children high moral and ethical values, faithfully attended church services, and often studied her Bible. To help prepare Andy to become a clergyman, Elizabeth sent him to a special academy that offered advanced subjects such as Latin and Greek and had higher standards than most frontier schools.

But, to his mother's disappointment, Andy didn't enjoy school. He often skipped class. He learned little of subjects such as science, history, and literature, and his spelling was terrible. Andy much preferred playing with his friends to studying. He was always ready for a wrestling match or a dare or a race on horseback. As a boy on the Crawford farm, Andy developed a love of horses, and he was an excellent rider. Tall, lean, strong, and agile, he was a natural athlete.

Despite his dislike for school, Andy was a good reader. Many people in that part of the country couldn't read at all. By the time Andy was nine, he was regularly chosen to

When he wasn't skipping class, Andy attended school in a small, crude cabin much like this one. Most frontier schools had only a single room, no windows, and logs for benches.

be a public reader when a newspaper arrived in town. People from local households, farms, and stores would gather around the handsome boy with the fiery red hair and listen intently as he read news of the outside world to them.

One of the most exciting newspaper articles that Andy read was about a meeting in Philadelphia, Pennsylvania, where colonists were discussing bold, revolutionary ideas. On a summer day in 1776, men, women, and children gathered around the nine-year-old boy and listened with rapt attention to the report of the Declaration of Independence that had been written by Thomas Jefferson of Virginia and passed by the Second Continental Congress. This was a moment that Andy never forgot. Declaring independence meant war with England!

News of the signing of the Declaration of Independence (above) spread throughout the colonies. Even in the remote Waxhaws, young Andy Jackson read from a newspaper proclaiming the event.

CHAPTER TWO

TEENAGE REVOLUTIONARY

"We hold these truths to be self-evident, that all men are created equal, that they are endowed by their Creator with certain unalienable Rights, that among these are Life, Liberty and the pursuit of Happiness."
—from the Declaration of Independence

The Declaration of Independence that Andy read in the Waxhaws set off the Revolutionary War between the American colonies and Britain. Thomas Jefferson and the other signers of the Declaration pledged their "Lives," their "Fortunes," and their "sacred Honor" to the cause of freedom. They knew that if the struggle for independence failed, they would lose everything.

Many colonists were willing to make the sacrifice. Ready to fight for their homes, their land, and a new, free nation—the United States of America—they enlisted in the Continental Army led by George Washington. General

With the signing of the Declaration of Independence came the American Revolution. As the fateful year of 1776 progressed, liberty-loving colonists from every walk of life enlisted in the Continental Army.

Washington's men were poorly supplied and untrained. They were a ragtag army pitted against the superior might of the large, disciplined, well-supplied British forces. The fight would be a fierce one.

Some colonists, called Tories, remained loyal to the British king. They joined the British in trying to put down the uprising. Andy and the other people living in the Waxhaws were fiercely independent and sided with Washington's American forces, or the Patriots. Most were eager to join in the struggle for freedom, especially young men and boys. Andy and his friends dreamed of winning honor, performing brave deeds, and proving themselves in battle. But for several years, the war had little effect upon the frontier, which was a long distance from the fighting. The boys of the Waxhaws had to satisfy their thirst for action with pranks and games.

An eager prankster himself, Andy Jackson was popular and fun loving. But even at a young age, he had a hot temper. He didn't take criticism well, and his emotions spilled over whenever anyone made fun of him. Once, when he was the butt of a joke by playmates, he shouted, with his piercing blue eyes ablaze, "By God, if one of you laughs, I'll kill him!"

They believed him. Andy was fun to be with, but he could be difficult and unpredictable. He was always ready for a fight when challenged, and he never backed down. Although Andy was usually the winner at foot racing, jumping, or horse racing, he was too thin and light to be good at wrestling. That didn't stop him from trying. A classmate remarked, "I could throw him three times out of four, but he would never *stay throwed.*"

WAR CREEPS CLOSER

While Andy was growing into a tall, lanky teenager, the Revolutionary War continued to rage in the northern and eastern colonies. So far, the British forces were beating the Patriots. In 1779 British troops marched into South Carolina.

THE ROAD TO REVOLUTION

When George III became the king of England in 1760, he was determined to strengthen the power of the monarchy throughout the British Empire. This empire included the American colonies. For a long time, Britain had not interfered much with these far-off possessions. The inhabitants of the colonies had developed habits of self-government and independence. They were angry when the British parliament, urged by the king, began to pass laws taxing the colonists and limiting their freedoms.

First, Parliament imposed a tax on molasses. A few years later, the Stamp Act required Americans to pay a tax for every newspaper, business paper, or other document that they used. This law was followed by the Townshend Acts, which charged tariffs, or taxes, on many imported products. Fierce opposition arose throughout the colonies. Colonists were angry that they had no voice in the British government. They called the laws "taxation without representation" and refused to pay.

The most violent protests took place in Boston in the colony of Massachusetts. The king punished these rebellious subjects by sending troops to patrol the Boston streets. This action only made the colonists angrier, especially in 1770 when these troops fired upon and killed several citizens during what came to be called the Boston Massacre. Until then, most colonists had considered themselves loyal subjects of the king. Their loyalty began to shift as the British continued to take action against the colonies.

In 1773 a group of determined Bostonians dressed as Indians boarded ships in Boston Harbor and tossed all the tea overboard. Tea was highly valued by the colonists, and it was also an item that had been heavily taxed by the Townshend Acts. After this protest, which became known as the Boston

On April 19, 1775, the "shot heard 'round the world" rang out in Lexington, Massachusetts. This skirmish between British and American troops was the first conflict of the American Revolution.

─────────────── ✦ ───────────────

Tea Party, King George took harsher measures than ever against the colony of Massachusetts, including a shelling of Boston by British warships. Representatives from all the colonies met at the First Continental Congress in Philadelphia in September 1774. They declared that they would support Massachusetts. In April 1775, British soldiers marched on Lexington, Massachusetts. A call went out to the Massachusetts militia (emergency armed forces), and conflicts with British forces took place at Lexington and nearby Concord. These were the first battles of the American Revolution.

The siege of Charleston, South Carolina, ended when the British captured the city on May 12, 1780. Andy's brother Hugh was one of more than two hundred American casualties.

———————— ◇ ————————

Andy's uncle, Robert Crawford, was put in charge of a militia to defend Charleston, South Carolina. Andy's sixteen-year-old brother, Hugh, was one of the volunteers under his command.

On May 12, 1780, Charleston fell to the British. It was a dark day. Hugh Jackson died, and the Jackson household was plunged into mourning.

War finally came to the Waxhaws as the British continued their push through the South. Dead and injured soldiers soon filled the straw-covered floor of Waxhaw Church, where Andy and his brother Robert helped their mother tend the wounded. A few weeks later, the British left the Waxhaws to concentrate on more important areas, but thirteen-year-old Andy was eager to fight the enemies who had invaded his land and killed his brother. He and Robert joined the South Carolina militia. Andy was given a pistol and made a messenger. He proudly described his duties as "a mounted orderly or messenger, for which I was well fitted being a good rider and knowing all the roads."

Andy put all his strength and energy into doing his job well. A teenaged girl living on a rural road recalled seeing the young messenger approach on horseback in a cloud of dust. When he came closer, she noticed that his broad-brimmed hat was torn and his legs were too long for the small horse he rode. When he was convinced that she, too, was a Patriot, the boy told her that his name was Andy Jackson. When she asked him about the American militia's progress against the British, he reported, "Oh, we are popping [fighting] them still."

CAPTURED!

Battles raged around the Waxhaws again. During a raid, the British set Waxhaw Church on fire and captured eleven American militiamen. Andy and Robert managed to escape. They scrambled through the woods and fields and hid out in the brush all night long. In the morning, they tried to

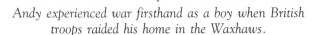

Andy experienced war firsthand as a boy when British troops raided his home in the Waxhaws.

find shelter in a nearby house, but it was the wrong place to seek help. British soldiers were inside. Andy and Robert were captured.

Even as a prisoner, Andy Jackson was proud and feisty. When he was ordered to clean a British officer's boots, Andy refused. He told the officer that he was a prisoner of war, not a servant. Furious, the officer drew his sword and slashed at the boy's head. Andy tried to defend himself against the blow, but the officer's sword cut Andy's fingers to the bone and left a deep gash on his head.

The British refused to give Andy medical treatment for his wounds, and he and his brother were marched forty miles to Camden, South Carolina. The captives were jammed into a prison with 250 other Patriot prisoners. Once a day, they were given a small, stale piece of bread

When Andy challenged a British officer, he took a blow that left scars that he carried all his life.

and a drink of water. There were no beds. Smallpox spread quickly through the filthy jail, and Andy and Robert were both infected. Suffering horribly, with no treatment available, they thought they would surely die.

But Andy's mother was as strong-willed as he was. When Elizabeth Jackson learned that her sons were in jail, she immediately rode to Camden. Elizabeth persuaded the commanding officer to release Andy, Robert, and several other Waxhaws boys.

The Jacksons made the miserable forty-mile journey home through a cold, nasty rainstorm. Robert was failing rapidly, and he was so sick and weak that he had to be tied onto his horse. Andy's shoes and coat had been stolen in prison, so he walked barefoot and coatless through the muddy downpour. The boys were barely clinging to life. Just two days after their return, Robert died. Another member of Andy's family was gone.

Andy, too, was deathly ill, and it looked as though he would soon follow his brother. His mother refused to give up. She nursed him tenderly for many months. Finally, though still weak, he was out of danger. "When it left me," he said of the smallpox, "I was a skeleton—not quite six feet long and a little over six inches thick! It took me all the rest of that year to recover my strength and get flesh enough to hide my bones."

ALONE

Elizabeth had saved the youngest of her three boys, but now she was needed elsewhere. American soldiers, including Elizabeth's nephews, were lying sick in British prison ships in Charleston Harbor, infected with "ship fever," or cholera.

Elizabeth Jackson's last days were spent in the hold of a British ship, nursing American prisoners of war who were sick with the deadly "ship fever."

———————————— ◇ ————————————

Elizabeth said good-bye to her son, advising him always to be loyal and honest to his friends. She also warned him, "never tell a lie, nor take what is not your own."

These were the last words that Andy would ever hear from his mother. In the autumn of 1781, Elizabeth Jackson traveled 160 miles to Charleston Harbor to nurse the suffering American prisoners. While ministering to the sick, she caught cholera herself. She died and was buried along with other victims of the disease in an unmarked grave near Charleston.

Back in the Waxhaws, fourteen-year-old Andy received a small bundle of his mother's clothes and the devastating news that she was gone. "I felt utterly alone," he said, "and tried to recall her last words to me."

Andy was an orphan.

CHAPTER THREE

FRONTIER SPIRIT

"... there was something about him I cannot
describe except to say that it was a presence.*"*
—Nancy Jarret

Soon after Elizabeth Jackson's death, in the winter of 1781, the fighting of the American Revolution ended with the surrender of the British at Yorktown, Virginia. The farmer-soldiers of the former colonies had beaten the most powerful army on earth. They had won independence for the United States of America.

Still weak from his bout with smallpox, Andy celebrated the American victory but grieved deeply for his mother and brothers. Without a real home or a stable, loving family, he moved around, living with various relatives. He spent a few months with an uncle, but the arrangement went badly. Andy was sullen, quick to take offense, and as hot-tempered as ever. He soon had a violent quarrel with another guest in the home, a militiaman named Captain Galbraith. After this unpleasant incident, Andy packed his meager

Patriots rejoiced at the news that British commander Lord
Cornwallis had surrendered his sword to George Washington at
Yorktown, Virginia, ending the fighting of the American Revolution.

————————————— ✧ —————————————

belongings and moved out of his uncle's house. He went to
live with a relative named Joseph White, where he got a job
as a saddler's apprentice. But Andy stayed only six months
before moving on again.

Growing up on the frontier had made Andy Jackson
tough and independent. He was one of a young, restless
breed, and as a teenager he spent most of his time with other
wild youngsters. They played cards, drank, and bet on horse
races and cockfights. His relatives sighed and shook their

heads, but Andy was uncontrollable. "No boy ever lived who liked fun better than he," said one of his acquaintances.

Andy's fun had a price. He gambled away more than he won and was soon in debt. Then, as though a pot of gold had fallen at his feet, his grandfather in Ireland left him an inheritance of several hundred pounds—a sum that was a small fortune to a boy with almost nothing. Andy collected the money in Charleston, accompanied by rowdy friends. He moved into an elegant hotel and bought expensive clothes. In a spree of drinking and gambling, he managed to lose his entire inheritance.

A LUCKY THROW

Andy Jackson was in deep trouble. He owed money everywhere and was at risk of going to prison for his debts. In desperation, he bet his only valuable possession—his horse—on a dice game called Rattle and Snap. Andy won the throw and came away with just enough to pay back the money that he owed.

This close call with disaster taught fifteen-year-old Andy a lesson. The game he won in Charleston was the last game of dice he ever played.

Andy rode home to the Waxhaws with a new determination to succeed. Not sure just what he wanted to do, he decided to try being a schoolteacher. He went back to school to complete the basic studies that he needed and taught school in the Waxhaws for about a year.

But the opportunities for a schoolmaster were limited, and Andy's energy and determination made him want more. He was seventeen years old and eager to make something important of his life. In search of new opportunities, he gathered his belongings and the money he had saved from his teacher's salary and left the Waxhaws in 1784.

A NEW FRONTIER

Salisbury, North Carolina, was seventy-five miles from Andrew Jackson's home. When seventeen-year-old Jackson mounted his horse and set out north, he put the Waxhaws and his childhood firmly into his past.

As the county seat of Rowan County, Salisbury's principal business was the handling of legal and political matters, and many of its most important citizens were lawyers. The law was a respected profession and a promising field for ambitious youths like Jackson. At that time, it was not necessary to attend college or law school in order to become an attorney. Most young men who hoped to become lawyers studied with a licensed attorney for several years. When they finished their studies, they were given a test by several judges. If they passed, they earned their license to practice law.

Jackson applied to study with Spruce McCay, a prominent attorney in Salisbury. The tall, determined young man impressed McCay. Jackson had an intensity and a drive that seemed promising, so McCay took him on as an apprentice.

Jackson set out to master the law. For two years, he pored over law books and listened carefully to McCay's lectures. He learned important details by copying documents and legal papers. There were other duties that were not so pleasant, such as sweeping the office and running errands. But these chores were part of the life of an apprentice, and Jackson accepted them.

Jackson also found time for fun in Salisbury. He met a group of high-spirited young men, and it didn't take long for the lively, outgoing teenager from the Waxhaws to become their leader. Every night, after completing his work and studies, Jackson would meet his friends for a rowdy evening of partying and practical jokes. One of Jackson's friends described him as "the most roaring, rollicking, game-cocking, horse-racing, card-playing, mischievous fellow that ever lived in Salisbury."

Jackson was also a favorite with the girls. He was six feet and one inch tall, lean, and strong, with a mop of unruly auburn hair and striking blue eyes. Nancy Jarret was one of the young women whom he often saw at parties. "His ways and manners," she recalled, "were most captivating."

After spending two years with Spruce McCay, Jackson switched to the law office of John Stokes. Stokes was considered one of the best lawyers practicing in North Carolina. After studying with Stokes for six months, Jackson was tested by two judges. They found that he was qualified to practice law, and that he was "a person of unblemished moral character." On September 26, 1787, Jackson was admitted to the bar, a professional association of lawyers, and authorized to practice law in the state of North Carolina.

At twenty years old, Jackson had achieved his goal of becoming a lawyer. But true success still seemed out of reach. He drifted around North Carolina for about a year, handling small cases, but not finding quite enough law work on his own to make a living.

Jackson turned his attention to politics and the government, an area that seemed to promise more opportunities for an ambitious young lawyer. He contacted John McNairy, an old Salisbury friend and fellow student who had just been elected Superior Court judge for the Western

District of North Carolina. This huge, sparsely settled area reached westward to the Mississippi River. A government position was open for a lawyer to prosecute cases in the Western District, and McNairy offered the job to Jackson. The wilderness of the frontier held no terrors for someone who had grown up in the Waxhaws, and Jackson gladly accepted the post. It would give him a decent salary, a chance to build up his own law practice, and maybe even a chance for adventure.

THE WILD WESTERN DISTRICT

In April 1788, Judge John McNairy, Andrew Jackson, and several other young men seeking their fortunes rode out into the blue mist of the Allegheny Mountains. Their mission was to bring law and civilization to the untamed Western District. Jackson had everything he would need for the journey. His fine horse carried two pistols slung from the saddle, a sleek new rifle, and a pack containing his few belongings, which included a collection of law books. Trailed by their hunting dogs, the small group headed west. Their final destination was the frontier town of Nashville, two hundred miles away.

The first leg of the group's journey took them to the town of Jonesboro. The country between there and Nashville was dangerous for small parties, so they decided to settle in Jonesboro until they could find a larger group also heading west. With Jackson's wild youth seemingly behind him, he was building a reputation as a gentleman, a respected citizen, and an attorney. The district court was in session, and Jackson had many opportunities to argue cases and earn fees.

The lawyer for the opposing side in one of Jackson's cases was Colonel Waightstill Avery, a well-known and experienced attorney. Still new to the job, Jackson referred often to his law books. Avery was amused by Jackson's uncertainty, and jokingly commented on the young lawyer's reliance on the books.

Jackson's fiery temper flared at the teasing remarks. He ripped a page out of one of his books and scribbled a few angry lines to Avery. Then he stewed and raged all night. The next morning, he wrote to the colonel, challenging him to a duel. "My charector you have injured," he wrote,

────────────────── ✧ ──────────────────

Jackson's spelling and grammar were not perfect, but his intentions were clear when he challenged Avery to a duel in this letter.

Agust 12ᵗ 1788

Sir

When a mans feelings & charector are injured he ought to seek a speedy redress: you Rec'd a few lines from me yesterday & undoubtedly you under stand me My charector you have injured: and further you have Insulted me in the presence of a court and a larg audiance & therefore call upon you as a gentleman to give me satisfaction for the Same: and I further call upon you to give me an answer immediately without Equivocation and I hope you can do without dinner un-till the business done: for it is consistant with the charector of a gentleman when he Injures a man to make a spedy reparation: therefore I hope you will not fail in meeting me this day. from yⁿ &tt Sᵗ

Coll° Avery   Andw Jackson

Of this Evening after court.

"and further you have Insulted me. . . . I therefore call upon you as a gentleman to give me satisfaction."

Duels were commonly considered an honorable way for gentlemen to settle an argument. Avery had to accept Jackson's challenge. Otherwise, he would risk losing his position in society and business. The two lawyers met at sundown in a hollow north of town. Neither one really wished to injure the other. They fired their pistols harmlessly into the air—enough to satisfy the code of honor. Jackson and Avery shook hands and the matter was settled.

THE LAW COMES TO TOWN

In September 1788, Jackson's group joined a large party of settlers traveling west along the Cumberland Road. One night the group set up camp and went to sleep. Awakened by the hooting of an owl, Jackson woke up his companions and pointed out that the owl's calls sounded too evenly spaced to be coming from real owls. In this barely settled region, Indians sometimes attacked strangers on the land. Jackson was certain that unfriendly Indians were close at hand, and he persuaded the others to break camp. They ran off into the forest. The next day, they learned that another group of travelers who had come along later and camped in the same spot had been set upon and killed by a war party of Cherokee Indians. Jackson's sharp frontiersman's senses may have saved his life and the lives of his companions.

The group finally reached Nashville on October 26. In 1788 downtown Nashville consisted of two stores, two taverns, a distillery, and a courthouse. Houses, shacks, and tents were scattered about. The town did not look impres-

Being a lawyer in the West was no job for the timid. This painting shows Jackson armed and ready to uphold the law.

———————————— ◇ ————————————

sive, but Jackson could imagine its possibilities. Soon settlers would be pouring into this vast new land. The future held no limits for a clever young lawyer.

Meanwhile, Jackson had to face some immediate problems. The courthouse was a run-down log structure. Its doors and windows barely hung in their frames or lay in pieces on the floor. The rickety furniture was filthy. Outside the courthouse, an attitude of disrespect for the law reigned in Nashville. Debtors who refused to pay their debts had banded together and were running the town like a gang of outlaws. Judge McNairy and his twenty-one-year-old public prosecutor set to work to change that.

A month after his arrival, Jackson had enforced seventy legal orders against debtors, demanding that legitimate debts be settled at once. The lawbreakers, who had done things their own way for so long, were furious. One of them dared to stride up to the new prosecutor and deliberately step hard upon his foot. Jackson did not hesitate. He seized a block of wood and swung it at the man, knocking him to the ground.

It was clear to everyone that the rule of law had arrived in Nashville. The creditors who had begun to collect their debts were grateful. They begged Jackson to take on all of their other legal affairs in his private practice, and he soon had more business than he could handle. Many settlers who were short of cash paid their lawyer with property, and Jackson was on his way to becoming one of the biggest landowners in the territory. He was happy and successful. And he had met Rachel Donelson Robards.

CHAPTER FOUR

DEVOTION AND DUTY

". . . it is the duty of every citizen to do something for his country."
—Andrew Jackson

The Donelsons were the first family to settle in Nashville. Colonel John Donelson, along with his wife and eleven children, had moved west from Virginia and settled in the Cumberland Valley. There, together with a fellow settler, they established the town of Nashville.

By the time Jackson arrived in Nashville looking for a place to stay, Colonel Donelson had died and his children were grown. The widow Donelson offered to take Jackson in as a boarder, delighted to have a strong man in the house for protection. In return, Jackson got to live in one of the most elegant homes in town. Associating with the respected Donelson family was also certain to help his career, and he happily accepted the offer.

About the time that Jackson moved in, the youngest

Donelson daughter, Rachel, came home from Kentucky, where she had lived with her jealous, abusive husband, Lewis Robards. Before her marriage, Rachel had been the belle of Nashville. She was outgoing and high-spirited. A relation described her as "irresistible to men," with a "beautifully moulded form" and a face that was always "rippling with smiles and dimples."

But Rachel had been miserable with the possessive, moody Robards. He was furious with her if she so much as glanced at another man, and his jealousy led to bitter arguments. After the unhappiness of life with her husband, Rachel was delighted to find charming, fun-loving Jackson living in her mother's house. A boy who worked there said that Jackson was "always polite . . . particularly so to the beautiful Mrs. Robards."

Rachel enjoyed Jackson's company, but they were careful not to let their relationship develop beyond friendship. This didn't prevent the stormy Robards from growing suspicious of Jackson, and it was soon clear that Rachel's marriage was ending. She even left Nashville to go into hiding for a while, afraid that her husband might come after her. Eventually, Lewis Robards filed for divorce. Divorces were rare and took a long time to be legally approved. When the news reached Nashville that the divorce had finally been granted, Jackson was eager to tell Rachel that she was free and that he loved her. In August 1791, they were married.

SETTLING DOWN

After a short, blissful honeymoon in Natchez, Mississippi, the couple returned to Nashville to begin their life

*When Rachel's jealous husband, Lewis Robards, filed for
divorce, he claimed that Rachel had been unfaithful to him.*

─────────────────── ✧ ───────────────────

together. Their marriage had changed them both. Finding
such love and happiness brought Jackson's temper under
control. He seemed more considerate to everyone, especially to Rachel. He was deeply protective of her, and he
treated her with tenderness and devotion. Rachel, safe
and content at last, became quiet and dedicated to her
religion.

But two years later, in December 1793, the Jacksons
received terrible news. Lewis Robards's divorce from Rachel
had not become final until September 1793, two years after
she had married Jackson. Shocked to discover that their
marriage was not legal, Jackson and Rachel obtained a new

Rachel was high-spirited, charming, and fond of smoking a pipe—a habit that was not unusual for frontier women.

——————————— ✧

license in January 1794 and were married again by the local justice of the peace.

No one knows for sure whether or not Robards deliberately tricked the Jacksons. He may have been trying to damage their reputations. Whatever the reason for the mix-up, it had no effect upon the couple's love or their commitment to each other. Their friends, neighbors, and relatives accepted what had happened as an honest error. The community continued to respect and admire them.

Eager to continue building their future together, Rachel and Jackson moved to a 330-acre plantation near Nashville. In the meantime, Jackson's career was leaping forward. He administered the law firmly as public prosecutor and was also busy with his expanding law practice. He traveled extensively, going wherever he was needed to try cases. Sometimes he had to cross flooded rivers or travel through wild or dangerous country. The men he traveled with on some of these journeys described him as "bold, dashing, fearless"—hardly a surprise for the man who, since his boyhood days of wrestling, had never backed down from a challenge.

Jackson's reputation and career were rising rapidly. He had a loving marriage and a comfortable home, and he was making more money and acquiring more land than the rebellious youngster from the Waxhaws would ever have dreamed possible.

PLANTATIONS AND POLITICS

The fertile land of the Western District was perfect for farming. The Jacksons grew cotton on their plantation. Like most Southern plantation owners at that time, they owned slaves to work the fields. Many Americans believed that slavery was immoral, but Jackson and most other Southerners saw nothing wrong with it. Slave labor made it possible for plantation owners to become rich growing cotton.

Jackson's work took him away from home so much that running the plantation became Rachel's responsibility. She was clever and efficient, and she was good at overseeing the details of the household and farm. Jackson doted on Rachel. He gave her full credit for their success as landowners.

Looking for success of their own, more pioneers came traveling across the mountains to settle. The population of the Western District grew so large that many people, including Andrew Jackson, proposed making the territory a separate state of the United States, also called the Union. A population count taken in 1795 showed that the region had enough people to qualify for statehood. But first it needed a constitution.

Jackson was chosen as a delegate to a state constitutional convention. He helped draw up the first draft of a constitution for the new state, which was named Tennessee. The Constitution of Tennessee was adopted in February

1796. On June 1, Tennessee became the sixteenth state admitted to the Union.

Tennessee's first governor was a popular Revolutionary War hero named John Sevier. The new state also needed to elect two senators and one representative to the U.S. Congress. William Blount, the former territorial governor, was elected to the Senate. Impressed by Jackson's forceful personality and down-to-earth manner, Blount persuaded him to run for the U.S. House of Representatives. He won easily.

Philadelphia, Pennsylvania, was the country's capital at the time. Congressman Andrew Jackson arrived there in December 1796. He was twenty-nine years old.

——————————— ✧ ———————————

The busy city streets of Philadelphia were a new experience for Jackson when he arrived from Tennessee in 1796.

THE YOUNG CONGRESSMAN

The nation was still new. George Washington, its first president, was just completing his second term. In a world dominated by monarchies, the United States of America was an experiment in democracy. Not everyone thought it could work, but Jackson firmly believed in democracy. He was determined to do whatever he could to help it survive and grow.

For all his commitment, Jackson, the frontiersman, stood out in a Congress that consisted mostly of wealthy East-

George Washington (above) was president when Jackson was elected to Congress.

─────── ✧ ───────

erners. One member of the House described him as "a tall, lank, uncouth-looking personage, with long locks of hair hanging over his face . . . his manners and deportment those of a rough backwoodsman."

Jackson attended sessions and voted dutifully in the House of Representatives, but he did not speak up very often. The new member of Congress had little experience in politics. He watched the proceedings quietly but closely, learning about national politics and observing how things were done.

He also missed Rachel. Leaving her had been hard.
"Attend . . . my Dear little Rachael. . . . If she should want
for anything [get] it for her," he told his brother-in-law.
Near the end of his term, he wrote to Rachel:

> My Dearest Heart
> With what pleasing hopes I view the future
> when I shall be restored to your arms there
> to spend My days . . . with you the Dear
> Companion of my life, never to be separated
> from you again . . . I mean to retire from . . .
> publick life.

Jackson hurried home when the session of Congress
ended in March 1797. But the following autumn, one of
Tennessee's seats in the U.S. Senate became available.
Although he was reluctant to leave Rachel again, Jackson felt
it was his duty to run for election as a senator. He won. This
time, he arrived in Congress wearing a well-fitted black coat
with a velvet collar, made to order by a Philadelphia tailor.

Jackson may have learned the importance of dressing
properly, but he still had more lessons to learn about political life. It was hard for him to control his temper when he
believed in something passionately. Thomas Jefferson
remarked that Jackson "could never speak on account of the
rashness of his feelings. I have seen him attempt it repeat-
edly, and as often choke with rage."

Jackson felt frustrated in the Senate, and Rachel was
unhappy about the time he had to spend in the capital. He
longed to be with her, too. Before long, he was also troubled
by financial worries caused by unsuccessful land deals.

Jackson resigned his Senate seat in 1798 and went home to try to earn enough from his legal practice to repay his debts.

JUDGE JACKSON TAKES THE BENCH

Back in Nashville, Jackson was elected as a judge of the Superior Court of Tennessee. This job was more to his liking than his work in Congress. It required him to travel around Tennessee, but he would never have to be away from Rachel for long.

Jackson was a popular and respected judge. Unlike many less formal judges, he wore a long black robe whenever he presided over a courtroom to emphasize the dignity of the law, even on the frontier. He instructed juries to "do what is *right*. . . that is what the law always *means*." His decisions were quick and simple. If action was required, Andrew Jackson never hesitated.

One defendant in Judge Jackson's courtroom got a first-hand taste of his decisive, fearless nature. Russell Bean, a hard-drinking bully, was on trial for the brutal crime of cutting off his own baby's ears. Bean cursed at the judge and jury and stormed out of the courtroom. On Judge Jackson's orders, the sheriff tried to arrest the man, but Bean frightened off the sheriff by threatening to shoot the "first skunk that came within ten feet." The sheriff retreated. Furious at Bean's disrespect for the law, Jackson rose from his bench and went after Russell Bean himself. Holding two deadly looking pistols, Jackson fixed his icy gaze on the man and ordered, "Surrender, you infernal villain, this very instant, or I'll blow you through."

Suddenly meek, Bean dropped his gun. Later he explained why he had given in. "I looked him in the eye,"

A defeated Russell Bean hangs his head in the face of Jackson's wrath.

——————— ✧ ———————

he said of Jackson, "and I saw shoot . . . and so I says to myself . . . it's about time to sing small, and so I did."

Even with his unconventional methods, Jackson earned a reputation as one of the best judges in Tennessee. People thought his decisions were honest, fair, and just.

At thirty-five years old, Jackson enjoyed being a judge, but he had another ambition. For many years, he had sought the honor of becoming major general of the Tennessee militia. He got his chance when elections for the post were held in 1802. The election ended with a tie between Jackson and his opponent, John Sevier, the former governor of Tennessee. The state's new governor, Archibald Roane, broke the tie in Jackson's favor.

*Rivalry between John Sevier (right)
and Jackson erupted in arguments,
insults, and finally a face-off.*
———————————————— ✧

John Sevier did not take defeat
well. Calling Jackson a "petty fog-
ging Lawyer," he seethed with
resentment. Sevier's dislike for
Jackson only increased when
Sevier decided to run for governor
again. Jackson supported Sevier's
opponent, and he exposed to the
public a land fraud scheme
involving Sevier. Sevier won the election in spite of these
disclosures—but he held onto his anger at Jackson.

A LADY'S HONOR

One day in 1803, Sevier was speaking to a crowd in a public square outside the courthouse in Knoxville, Tennessee.
Judge Jackson was in town to hear cases, and when he
appeared in the square, Sevier turned on him with an
insult. To defend himself, Jackson pointed out his own services to the public.

Sevier hooted at this. "Services?" he shouted, "I know
of no great service you have rendered the country, except
taking a trip . . . with another man's wife."

Jackson flew into a rage at this reference to Rachel and
to their marriage. "Do you mention *her* sacred name?" he
demanded. The two men were about to battle right there in
the square, until onlookers separated them.

Always prepared for a fight, Jackson had his own pair of dueling pistols.

——————————— ◇ ———————————

But Jackson could not forget or forgive an insult to his beloved Rachel. His devotion to her had only grown stronger over the years. He promptly sent Sevier a message challenging him to a duel.

"You . . . took the sacred name of a lady in your polluted lips. . . . I Andrew Jackson, do pronounce, publish, and declare to the world, that . . . John Sevier . . . is a base coward."

Sevier accepted the challenge. Dueling was against the law in Tennessee but still legal in Kentucky, so the two men met in a field just across the border. They shouted insults at each other and drew their pistols. But before the enemies could hurt each other, their friends persuaded them to put away their weapons and leave.

The duel with John Sevier had ended harmlessly. Jackson had protected his own name as a fearless man of honor, and he had defended his dear Rachel.

CHAPTER FIVE

REPUTATIONS AND RIVALRIES

"[Andrew Jackson] knew his own mind. . . .
he would do what he said he would."
—Dr. Felix Robertson of Nashville, Tennessee

In 1801 Thomas Jefferson had become president of the United States. One of his first accomplishments after taking office was negotiating the Louisiana Purchase. This agreement with France added a large expanse of new western territory to the United States. Jackson, who was a loyal supporter of the president, was pleased with Jefferson's decision to buy the land. "All the Western Hemisphere," he wrote to President Jefferson, "rejoices at the Joyfull news."

Eager to be part of the nation's growth, Jackson asked Jefferson to appoint him governor of the new territory. When the president chose another man for the post, Jackson felt insulted and deeply humiliated. His pride was wounded, and he began to oppose Jefferson's policies.

IN BUSINESS

Jackson was disappointed that Jefferson hadn't given him the job as governor, but his career as a judge was going well. In 1804, however, it became necessary for him to resign. Once again, he needed time to attend to his financial problems. Jackson's public service didn't bring in very much money, and it had taken time away from his legal practice. He had to sell off a large part of his landholdings, including his and Rachel's home, to pay off debts. With the money that was left over, he and Rachel bought a new home, called the Hermitage.

The Hermitage began as a modest group of log buildings. While the couple worked to develop the land into a profitable plantation, Jackson also tried to make money in

The first Hermitage farmhouse (shown here ca. 1880), where Jackson lived from 1804 to 1821, was originally a stately, two-story log farmhouse. After Jackson moved into a more substantial brick home in 1821, the first floor was removed and the farmhouse became slave quarters.

other businesses. He bought a machine called a cotton gin to remove the seeds from harvested cotton, and he invested in stores that sold rifles, coffee, cotton, and tobacco.

Jackson also bought a racetrack and his own racehorse. Since his days on his uncle's farm, he had never lost his love of horses. He named his new horse Truxton, trained him himself, and entered him in competitions. Truxton went on to win many races, and the money Jackson won helped ease his financial problems. The victories also earned him a reputation as an expert on horses, and the racetrack prospered.

As time went on, the plantation at the Hermitage became more profitable, too. Rachel managed the farm, which produced valuable crops of cotton, corn, and wheat. Things were going well for the Jacksons.

HORSE RACES AND HOTHEADS

While the plantation flourished, Jackson's prized horse, Truxton, also continued to earn money for Jackson. In 1806 Truxton beat a horse called Ploughboy in a highly publicized race. Charles Dickinson, the son-in-law of Ploughboy's owner, published an insulting article about Jackson, calling him "a worthless scoundrel, a poltroon [another word for "coward"] and a coward."

It was always a mistake to insult Jackson. Temper high, he immediately sent Dickinson a challenge to meet him in a duel.

Dickinson accepted. On May 29, 1806, Andrew Jackson got up before dawn. He left Rachel, telling her that he might be gone for a few days due to some trouble with Charles Dickinson.

THE HERMITAGE

The Hermitage (above) was Andrew Jackson's home for forty years. He and Rachel bought 425 acres of land near Nashville, Tennessee in 1804. They gradually added to the property, and by 1845 the estate included 1,000 acres, a beautiful home, outbuildings, stables, and a large plantation. Slaves worked in the house and on the farm. Cotton, the main crop, was grown and processed on the plantation. It was then sent by boat to New Orleans, Louisiana, to be sold.

The Hermitage was more than just a house and farm to Jackson. It was the only place where his restless spirit felt calm. He and Rachel shared many happy times in this home. "How often," he once remarked yearningly, "do my thoughts lead me back to The Hermitage."

The home of America's seventh president is a national historic landmark. The residence contains original furniture, wallpaper, and portraits. Jackson's personal possessions are also displayed, including eyeglasses, his sword, and a Bible. Visitors from around the world can see Andrew Jackson's Hermitage just as it was during his lifetime.

Charles Dickinson was known as one of the best shots in Tennessee. He boasted that he would kill Andrew Jackson with the first shot. When he left his own house that morning, he confidently told his pregnant wife, "I shall be sure to be at home to-morrow evening."

Jackson and Dickinson met on the banks of the Red River in Kentucky. The two men took positions eight paces apart. They paced off in opposite directions, then turned to face each other.

General Thomas Overton, an acquaintance of Jackson's, acted as his second, his assistant in the duel. When the opponents had taken their places, he asked, "Gentlemen, are you ready?"

Both men said that they were.

General Overton called out for the duelers to shoot. Dickinson raised his pistol and fired. Jackson wobbled and clutched his chest. He had been struck by Dickinson's bullet. For a moment, Jackson thought he was dying. He gritted his teeth against the pain. With all his willpower, he forced himself to stand upright.

"My God! Have I missed him?" Dickinson exclaimed. He couldn't believe what was happening, but the rules forced him to stand his ground and wait for Jackson's shot.

Jackson pointed his pistol at his opponent and squeezed the trigger. Nothing happened. The gun hadn't fired. He aimed and shot again, and Dickinson fell to the ground.

At that moment, General Overton noticed that blood was pouring from Jackson's chest. "I believe that he pinked me," Jackson muttered, "but I don't want those people to know." Later Jackson would say, "I should have hit him [even] if he had shot me through the brain."

This illustration of the Dickinson duel shows Jackson knocked to the ground by Dickinson's bullet.

◇

Despite his boastful words, Jackson had been gravely wounded. Two of his ribs were cracked, and the bullet from Dickinson's gun was lodged in his chest, so close to his heart that it could not safely be removed.

Charles Dickinson was in even worse condition. Jackson's bullet had passed through his body, leaving a gaping hole. He tossed in agony the rest of the day. That night, he bled to death.

When Rachel heard the news, she wept. "Oh, God have pity on the poor wife," she prayed, and "on the babe in her womb."

At first many people in Nashville criticized Jackson for Dickinson's tragic death. But dueling was still an accepted part of frontier culture, and Jackson's reputation did not suffer for long. His health, on the other hand, did suffer. Almost a month passed before he could move around without enormous pain. But Jackson forced himself to get back to work as soon as possible. He had a business to attend to and a plantation to run.

There was still one thing missing from the Jacksons' life. Both of them longed to have a family, but they were unable to have children of their own. In 1809 Rachel's sister-in-law gave birth to twins. Too weak and ill to care for both babies, the mother put one of them into Rachel's care. She and Jackson adopted the child and named him Andrew Jackson Jr. Delighted to have a child at last, the Jacksons enjoyed a time of quiet togetherness at the Hermitage.

CHAPTER SIX

THE GENERAL

"Your General . . . knows the valor of the men he commands. . . . With his soldiers he will face all dangers, and with them participate in the glory of conquest."
—Colonel John Coffee,
one of Andrew Jackson's officers

Life at the Hermitage was peaceful, but Jackson knew that trouble was brewing in other parts of the United States. For years the United States had been having difficulties with Great Britain. The British refused to respect American independence and kept trying to regain their control over the former colonies. They seized American ships on the high seas. They kidnapped thousands of American sailors and forced them into service to the British king. They encouraged Native American tribes to make raids upon American settlers.

The Americans had their own plans. They wanted to expand their young nation westward into Indian lands, and

*Although he did not have much military experience, Jackson was eager to
lead his troops against enemies of the United States of America.*

southward into Spanish-owned Florida. They even hoped to
take over parts of the British colonies to the north of the
United States, in the area that would become Canada.
British interference threatened to ruin all of these plans, and
hotheaded congressmen called for war against Britain. These
congressmen included Henry Clay of Kentucky and John C.
Calhoun of South Carolina. They called themselves the War
Hawks, and they were eager to teach Britain a lesson.

In Tennessee, Jackson was on fire with this same desire to
fight for his country. As the major general of Tennessee's militia, he was ready to lead his men into battle. He did not

have much military experience, but he was known to be courageous, loyal, and decisive. The soldiers he commanded trusted him. Although he had offered his services during several minor conflicts, they were always settled before he could participate. Nevertheless, he sent out a call for volunteer soldiers. "Shall we, who have clamoured for war, now skulk into a corner?" he asked scornfully. "No, we are the free born sons of . . . the only republick now existing in the world."

James Madison had succeeded Thomas Jefferson as president in 1809. Like his fellow citizens, he was angered by British raids on American ships and sailors. He declared war upon England on June 1, 1812. Two weeks later, Congress approved this decision.

The War of 1812 finally gave Jackson the chance to prove himself as a general. As soon as he heard that war had broken out, he offered the services of the Tennessee militia, troops consisting of 2,500 young men whom Jackson had trained himself. He had confidence in their ability and courage. But the secretary of war ignored the offer for many months, and other generals were given the assignments that Jackson wanted. Jackson was furious. He had a "holy zeal for the welfare of the

————————————— ✧
President James Madison

United States," said his friend, Governor William Blount. Determined to be prepared for battle when it did come, Jackson purchased rifles with money from his own pocket and continued to train his troops.

OLD HICKORY

In late 1812, the war was going badly for the Americans. The British captured many U.S. cities, while Jackson waited with growing impatience for an assignment. Months of idleness were dampening his spirits, as well as those of his troops.

Finally, their chance came. The War Department sent a request to Governor Blount to send reinforcements to New Orleans, Louisiana. In December 1812, Blount appointed Andrew Jackson a major general of the U.S. Army and asked him to bring his troops to New Orleans.

Jackson and Tennessee's volunteer militiamen assembled on the banks of the Cumberland River on an icy winter day, ready to board flatboats for the first leg of their journey. People watched from the shore, cheering and waving.

Before leaving, Jackson sent an affectionate letter to Rachel at the Hermitage. "My Love," he wrote, "We part but for... a few fleeting weeks when the protecting hand of Providence ... will restore us to each other's arms."

The day was freezing, and the men were not supplied for such unusually cold weather. Jackson equipped them as well as he could. One citizen who was watching the embarkment criticized Jackson for not being better prepared. "Let me hear no more such talk," roared Major General Jackson, "or... [I'll] ram that red hot handiron down your throat."

Jackson and his men sailed down the Cumberland, Ohio, and Mississippi Rivers. It took them thirty-nine days to reach Natchez, Mississippi. There they found orders instructing them to stay in Natchez, as there were no supplies for them in New Orleans.

They set up a rough camp and waited. Weeks later, in February 1813, orders came from the secretary of war. "The causes for embodying . . . the Corps under your command having ceased to exist, you will . . . consider it dismissed from public service."

After traveling eight hundred miles under difficult winter conditions, Jackson and his soldiers were being told to turn around and go home. Jackson seethed and raged against the unfair way he and his troops had been treated. His men had run out of rations. They were hungry, weak, and cold. Many were ill, but they had no medical supplies.

Jackson did not intend to abandon his loyal men. He notified the secretary of war that he would not obey the command to dismiss his troops and leave them to manage on their own. He would lead them home himself. After borrowing money to buy wagons and supplies, General Jackson and his ragged militia began the long march home. Jackson gave up his own horse so that it could carry young men who were sick. He ordered his officers to do the same. The general walked alongside his mare. He spoke to the weary men, encouraging them and trying to keep their spirits up with stories and jokes. The soldiers were grateful for his kindness. They admired his courage and compared him to the strongest hardwood they knew—hickory. Their tribute to their tough but compassionate commander was a nickname that would stick. They called him Old Hickory.

In addition to earning the devotion of his soldiers, Jackson's courage and dedication to his men brought him the admiration of the public. A Nashville newspaper applauded the local hero. "Long will their General live in the memory of his volunteers of West Tennessee for his benevolence, humane, and fatherly treatment to his soldiers," they wrote. "If gratitude and love can reward him, General Jackson has them."

THE BENTON BROTHERS

Back in Tennessee, Jackson waited for new orders. In the meantime, he got involved in a conflict closer to home. Billy Carroll and Jesse Benton, two young men in Nashville, were set to face off in a duel. Jackson reluctantly agreed to act as Carroll's second. During the duel, Benton was embarrassingly wounded in the buttocks and became an object of

Jackson (fourth from left) is depicted in his fight with the Bentons in this humorous illustration. The duel made big news in Nashville.

ridicule around town. His brother, Thomas Hart Benton, was upset with Jackson for not preventing the fight. He sent Jackson an angry letter and said insulting things about him to friends and acquaintances in Nashville.

Jackson was furious at this tarnishing of his reputation. By the time he bumped into the Benton brothers on a street in Nashville, both sides were ready for a fight. Jackson strode toward Thomas, threatening to horsewhip him. Thomas reached for his weapon, but Jackson drew his pistol first and began to back Thomas into a corner. Coming to his brother's rescue, Jesse pulled out his own gun and fired at Jackson, shattering his shoulder with one bullet and piercing his arm with another. Friends of Jackson's rushed into the battle, brandishing guns and swords, but bystanders stopped the fight and carried Jackson, who was bleeding heavily, into a hotel. The doctors who examined him wanted to amputate his arm, but Jackson, barely conscious, stubbornly insisted, "I'll keep my arm."

Jackson was so weak from the injury and the massive loss of blood that he could not get out of bed for three weeks. He did keep his arm, but he also kept one of Jesse Benton's bullets. It was so close to the bone that doctors didn't dare try to remove it. At forty-six years old, Jackson had another bullet lodged in his body.

THE CREEK WAR

Jackson had not fully recovered from his latest wound when he received orders to lead his troops against the Creek Indians. Hoping to weaken the Americans, the British and the Spanish had encouraged the Creeks to revolt. Partly in an effort to keep their land from being taken by white set-

The attack on Fort Mims enraged American settlers and gave them an excuse to go to war against the Creek Indians.

———————————— ✧ ————————————

tlers, many Indians agreed to fight. Led by Chief Red Eagle, Creek warriors called Red Sticks killed hundreds of American settlers at Fort Mims in present-day Alabama. When the news reached Tennessee, the public was outraged. General Jackson, still pale and weak, dragged himself from his sickbed. He called for volunteers to avenge the slain settlers. "Those distressed citizens of that frontier... implored the brave Tennesseans for aid," he exclaimed. "They must not ask in vain."

In October 1813, Jackson and his troops moved against the Creeks. A long and bloody war followed. Hundreds of Native Americans were killed. Jackson and his soldiers kept running out of supplies. Jackson himself was weak from his

General Jackson guided his soldiers with a firm hand. When his troops threatened to desert during the Creek War, Jackson aimed his rifle and forced them back.

———————————————— ◇ ————————————————

recent injury, as well as from an uncomfortable intestinal disease called dysentery. His men were hungry, and many of them were ill. The situation was so bad that some soldiers tried to desert the army. The general's compassion for his men did not extend to deserters. He had one of them tried by a military court and shot as an example to the rest of the troops.

The Creek War ended in victory for the U.S. Army in March 1814 at the Battle of Horseshoe Bend. Chief Red

Eagle and his warriors surrendered to General Jackson, whom they called Sharp Knife. Jackson insisted that the Creeks sign a treaty that took away most of their land. Like most Americans of his time, Jackson viewed Native Americans as savages. He did not believe that they had any rights of ownership over the lands on which they lived.

Jackson was hailed as a hero for his success in the Creek War. On all other fronts, the War of 1812 was still going badly for the Americans. On August 24, 1814, the British marched on Washington, D.C. They set fires that damaged the Capitol and the President's House, along with other public buildings and many homes. With the cooperation of the Spanish, British troops assembled in Florida

————————— ✧ —————————

Flames lit the sky over Washington, D.C., on August 24, 1814, after British troops captured and set fire to the city.

to prepare for an assault on New Orleans. The British were also training thousands of Native Americans in the Spanish territory of Florida to fight against American troops. Although they were aware of the threat, U.S. leaders were reluctant to invade an area controlled by Spain. Andrew Jackson did not hesitate. He marched his troops to Pensacola, Florida. Taking the enemy by surprise, he demanded and received the surrender of the city, weakening British influence there.

Jackson was pleased with this success, but he was hungry for more. Expecting a British invasion of New Orleans, he traveled there to prepare for another battle.

THE HERO OF NEW ORLEANS

New Orleans was a prize that the British wanted badly. It was an important port, and Jackson was determined to preserve it for the United States. He had always wanted an opportunity to prove his courage and ability as a leader and defend the nation he loved. The British had been responsible for the loss of his brothers and mother. Now they were threatening his world again.

General Jackson and his troops entered New Orleans on December 1, 1814. Jackson found a city completely helpless and open to attack. There were no stocks of arms or supplies. No preparations had been made for defense.

Jackson immediately took charge, drawing the attention and curiosity of local residents. One of them described Jackson as "a tall, gaunt man, very erect . . . with a countenance furrowed by care and anxiety. His dress was simple and nearly threadbare. . . . His complexion was sallow and unhealthy; his hair iron grey, and his body thin and emaciated. . . . But . . . [a] fierce glare . . . [lighted] his bright and hawk-like eye." New Orleans society whispered about the "wild General from Tennessee." When they entertained him at dinner, they were surprised to discover that he was a well-spoken, courtly gentleman. One guest exclaimed to her hostess, "Is this your back woods-man? Why, madam, he is a prince."

The general had things on his mind other than the opinions of society ladies. Most people believed that the superior British forces were certain to capture New Orleans. Andrew Jackson was determined not to let that happen. He surveyed the city and surrounding areas and considered battle strategies. He set crews to work cutting down trees, using them to clog waterways leading to the city and to block the approach of British ships. Earthen ramparts were built along the canals, behind which defending soldiers could take cover. To keep order within the city, General Jackson declared military law and put a curfew into effect.

Meanwhile, the general began to put together the forces that would defend the city. Men flocked into New Orleans to fight for Old Hickory. Among these were riflemen and scouts from Mississippi, Alabama, and Louisiana. A group of Choctaw Indians joined forces with the militiamen. Residents of New Orleans, including African Americans who were classified as "free men of color," took up rifles to protect their city. Jackson even reluctantly accepted the help of the local pirates. Led by the legendary cutthroat Jean Laffite, these "hellish banditti" had a reputation as excellent fighters.

Two weeks after Jackson's arrival, a fleet of British ships arrived at Lake Borgne, one of the many waterways near

General Jackson, astride a white horse, offered his troops leadership and support during the fierce fighting of the Battle of New Orleans in 1815.

——————————————— ✧ ———————————————

the city. The British ships exchanged gunfire with American boats on the lake. The Battle of New Orleans had begun.

It lasted for many weeks. In the first skirmishes, the advantage went back and forth between the British and the Americans. The British had more soldiers and were better disciplined, but the Americans were more resourceful at fighting backwoods-style. They surprised the enemy by silently creeping up on them through the brush and muddy waters. They hid in the swamps and bayous (marshy, slow-moving waterways) until the British came in sight and then fired upon them from their hiding places.

On New Year's Day 1815, the main British force, numbering about seven thousand men, closed in to face three thousand Americans. The troops met just outside of the

city of New Orleans. "I will smash them," General Jackson
thundered, "so help me God!"

The British began to bombard the American forces
using Congreve rockets. These balls of fire landed with ear-
splitting shrieks, shaking the earth for miles around from
the terrifying force of their explosions.

Andrew Jackson calmed his men. "Don't mind these
rockets," he told them. "They are mere toys to amuse children." The British later admitted that the Americans were
the "first . . . army that was not thrown into confusion by
their rockets."

The Americans responded with their own fire. The
British could not break through the American lines, and
retreated to regroup their forces.

A week later, the scene was set for a dramatic battle.
Early on the morning of January 8, 1815, the British
attacked again. The American forces stood firm. General
Jackson seemed to be everywhere, directing the battle and
inspiring the men with his own confidence and optimism.
He strode back and forth among the soldiers, helping and
encouraging them. At one point, he stood upon a high
plateau. From there he could see the entire battle. He
watched calmly as his forces steadily mowed down the
advancing British. Under unrelenting fire, the British finally retreated in a disorderly rout.

On January 8, there were approximately two thousand
British casualties. Only seventy-one of Jackson's men were
dead, missing, or wounded. The Battle of New Orleans had
ended in a decisive victory for the Americans.

A great celebration was held in New Orleans. Crowds
gathered in the streets, on balconies, and in the square in

front of the city's cathedral. They cheered wildly when General Jackson rode into the square. A crown of laurel leaves was set upon the head of the forty-seven-year-old general. Girls threw flowers at his feet as the church bells rang.

Although no one knew it until later, the War of 1812 had officially ended before the Battle of New Orleans. A peace treaty had been signed in Ghent, Belgium, two weeks earlier. But news traveled slowly then, and no one on the American side of the Atlantic Ocean knew about the treaty. Word of the victory at New Orleans and news of the peace treaty reached Washington, D.C., at the same time.

Nevertheless, Jackson's great accomplishment was the pride of the peole in the United States. He was hailed as a national hero. In Washington, crowds cheered in the streets. A columnist for *Niles' Weekly Register* wrote, "Glory be to God that the barbarians have been defeated. . . . Glory to Jackson." The *New York Evening Post* declared, "If we had a Jackson everywhere we should succeed everywhere."

Congress thanked Jackson for his service and awarded him a gold medal. President James Madison sent a message saying, "History records no example of so glorious a victory . . . with so little bloodshed on the part of the victorious." Songs were even written about Jackson.

Andrew Jackson had become a national legend. Forever after he would be known as the hero of New Orleans. His brilliant victory had demonstrated to the British once and for all that they no longer had any power over their former colonies. America was respected by nations in all parts of the world.

HOME TO THE HERMITAGE

When Jackson traveled home to Tennessee, he was greeted along the route by adoring crowds. John Reid, the general's aide, described his reception. "He is everywhere hailed as the saviour of this Country. . . . women, children, & old men line the road to look at him." Jackson received the attention graciously. "He pulls off his hat," Reid wrote, and "bows."

In Nashville everybody came out to greet the hometown hero. He was escorted into town by a procession of enthusiastic supporters. Jackson responded by saying, "I am at a loss to express my feelings. The approbation of my fellow-citizens is to me the richest reward."

Jackson had paid a price to become a hero. Months of strenuous activity despite constant illness and pain had left him in bad health. But Jackson was overjoyed to be home with Rachel and their family. Over the years, he and Rachel had fulfilled their desire for a family by raising children who needed homes. The children in the Jackson household included Andrew Jackson Jr., a Creek boy named Lyncoya, and other relatives and wards whom the couple had taken in at the Hermitage. Jackson settled down at the Hermitage into the life of a successful plantation owner. He was forty-eight years old.

After the end of the War of 1812, the U.S. Army reorganized into northern and southern divisions. Major General Andrew Jackson was put in command of the southern division, an arrangement that enabled him to use the Hermitage as his headquarters. Rachel was happy to have her family living together in her beloved home, and she hoped that their comfortable, domestic life would continue forever.

A Fellow Orphan

During the Creek War, Jackson found a Creek toddler alone on one of the bloody fields of battle. The child's family members had all been killed. There was no one to take him in or care for him. Despite his often harsh attitude toward Native Americans, Jackson felt a surge of sympathy for this boy, remembering how he, too, had been orphaned at an early age. He carried the youngster to his own tent and fed him. When the campaign ended, the child was sent to Rachel at the Hermitage. "I . . . want him well taken care of," Jackson told Rachel.

The Jacksons named the boy Lyncoya and raised him at the Hermitage. He was happy in the loving atmosphere of the household, where he and Andrew Jackson Jr. played together. As Lyncoya grew older, he also began to explore his Native American heritage.

Jackson took a strong interest in the education of all of his children. He had high hopes for Lyncoya and hoped to send him to West Point. But Lyncoya never saw that day. He became deathly ill with tuberculosis, and though Rachel cared for him lovingly, he died in his teens. Both Rachel and Jackson grieved over the loss of their son.

THE SEMINOLE CAMPAIGN

In the early 1800s, Florida was owned by Spain. Florida and the southeastern United States were home to the Seminoles, a nation made up of several Native American tribes. The Seminoles lived on land that was coveted by American settlers who were hungry for expansion. In the eyes of most Americans, including Andrew Jackson, the Indians stood in the way of progress. They simply had to go.

*Many Seminole Indians made their homes in small villages
such as this one in the Florida Everglades.*

As the military commander in charge of the southern United States, Jackson had the power to deal with the Indians. He wanted to seize all of Florida from the Spaniards and take the Seminoles' land, but he needed an excuse to lead a military expedition into Florida. James Monroe, who became president in 1817, could not order an outright invasion of Spanish territory without good cause. The rest of the world would condemn such an aggressive action. But Jackson felt sure that the capture of Florida was exactly what both he and the president wanted.

Jackson soon got his chance. U.S. troops had already entered Florida once, to destroy a fort held by runaway American slaves. U.S. soldiers and Indians also clashed frequently near Florida's border. In November 1817, American soldiers crossed the border again and attacked a Seminole settlement, killing many of the inhabitants and burning the village. The Indians took revenge by seizing a boat of American soldiers, women, and children, killing almost everyone aboard. Only a few people managed to escape. When news of this event reached newspapers around the country, public opinion against the Indians became more inflamed than ever.

It was exactly the excuse that President Monroe had been seeking. In December he ordered Jackson to move against the Seminoles, "a tribe which has long violated our rights, & insulted our national character."

General Jackson set off for Florida with several thousand soldiers and arrived there in March 1818. His troops occupied Spanish forts and used them as bases from which they

——————————————— ✧ ———————————————

The victories of Jackson and his troops in Florida, shown below capturing Pensacola, opened up the region to settlement by Americans.

*U.S. troops took Seminole chiefs hostage
during the campaign in Florida.*

✧

attacked and destroyed Seminole villages, killing anyone
who resisted. Jackson even executed two British men who
had been training the Indians. Some people were shocked
by the violence of the attacks on the Seminoles, but most
Americans approved of Jackson's actions.

A few months later, in May 1818, Jackson's troops occupied Pensacola. The Spanish had reclaimed this city after
the War of 1812 and used it as their capital in Florida, but
it was poorly defended. With this important city in their
grasp, the Americans finally had control over Spanish
Florida. Early in 1819, Spain signed a treaty agreeing to sell
Florida to the United States for five million dollars.
American settlers streamed across the border, eager to get
their share of this valuable land.

General Andrew Jackson was hailed yet again as a national hero. A Washington newspaper called his achievement "among the most important in the annals of our history." The grateful President Monroe offered him an appointment as governor of the new Florida territory.

Jackson accepted the president's offer, but he needed to rest first. As usual, he had put his military duty before his health, which had grown worse during the recent campaigns. "I am at present worn down with fatigue," he wrote President Monroe, "and by a bad cough with a pain in my left side which produced a spitting of blood . . . [and has] reduced me to a skelleton."

But after a short period of recuperation at the Hermitage, Jackson was anxious to be active once more. He resigned from the army, ready to begin an adventure as governor of a brand-new territory.

CHAPTER SEVEN

THE CANDIDATE

*". . . the people have a right to choose whom
they will to perform their constitutional duties,
and when the people call, the Citizen is bound
to render the service."*

—Andrew Jackson

In April 1821, Jackson set off for Florida with Rachel, Andrew Jackson Jr., and one of his wards, Andrew Jackson Hutchings, the orphaned child of a friend. Although Rachel wanted to be with her family, the idea of moving to a new territory miles away made her uneasy. She loved her home in Tennessee. She led a quiet life at the Hermitage and among her friends in Nashville.

As the years had passed, Rachel had changed from the high-spirited, fun-loving young woman she had been when she and Jackson first met. She had a great deal of responsibility running the household and plantation of the Hermitage. She didn't enjoy her husband's long absences,

Rachel supported Jackson's career, but she preferred her privacy to the public life demanded by politics.
✧ ——————————————————

but she loved taking care of their adopted children and helping others in the community. Religion was important to her, and she spent much time in prayer. She still had a warm smile, but she had grown quiet, serious, and rather plump.

When the Jacksons passed through New Orleans on their way to Florida, the people's pleasure-loving way of life shocked Rachel. Florida, too, seemed to be filled with evildoing. As soon as Jackson took charge in Pensacola, Rachel persuaded him to close the gambling houses and to prohibit dancing and music on the Sabbath.

Jackson had troubles of his own in Florida. His first task as governor was to make the transition from a Spanish to an American administration. The former Spanish governor, Colonel José Callava, was difficult to deal with. At first, he refused to meet with Jackson. Then he argued over every detail. At last he cooperated, and a ceremony took place, officially transferring control of the territory to the new American governor. The Spanish flag was lowered, and the Stars and Stripes were raised over the government house.

Although Jackson was ready to create a new government in Pensacola, it seemed that obstacles were placed in his path at every turn. Friends and acquaintances begged him for positions in the new government, but Jackson was denied the authority to make these decisions. President Monroe and members of his staff in Washington overruled Jackson and made their own selections.

Nevertheless, Jackson tried to use his powers as governor to promote justice for all. "I . . . ever will believe," he wrote in a letter to the secretary of state, "that just laws can make no distinction of privilege between the rich and poor. . . . the great can protect themselves, but the poor and humble, require the arm and shield of the law."

Jackson was accustomed to leading armies and having control over his campaigns. In Florida he was constantly frustrated by political disagreements and petty details. In

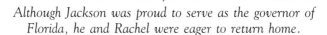

Although Jackson was proud to serve as the governor of Florida, he and Rachel were eager to return home.

spite of these handicaps, he accomplished as much as he could. He set up a simple, easy-to-run government in Pensacola. He mapped out county lines and established courts. He put laws into effect to promote public health.

When he had completed these tasks, Jackson decided that he was tired of Florida. The climate and food did not agree with him or with Rachel. They suffered from malaria and indigestion. The bullets lodged in Jackson's body became infected and painful. After fewer than eight months in Florida, he resigned the governorship as of December 1, 1821.

THE PEOPLE CALL

The Jacksons went home to Nashville. For several months, Jackson was too sick to do anything but rest. Rachel cared for him tenderly, and the couple's affection was stronger than ever. When Jackson's health improved, the couple began to entertain guests at the Hermitage. Rachel enjoyed being a hostess, and Jackson loved to engage in discussions on a wide range of subjects. The backwoods boy from the Waxhaws had become skilled at conversation. He listened attentively to others before stating his own positions clearly and convincingly.

Jackson also found time to follow national affairs. At that time, some politicians wanted a strong national government that favored the rich. Others, including Thomas Jefferson, were afraid of putting too much power in the hands of a central government. They believed it threatened the rights of ordinary people. In both parties, the method of choosing the next candidates for president had become corrupt. Newspapers had uncovered political scandals involving bribery and the misuse of power.

People talked about finding an honest, forceful man to run for president. Some of them turned to a national idol—Old Hickory. At first, Jackson showed no interest. "Do they think I am such a . . . fool!" he said. "I know what I am fit for. I can command a body of men in a rough way; but I am not fit to be President." He was also concerned about his family and children. He wanted to give them more time and attention.

But as scandals and corruption continued in Washington, D.C., Jackson worried about the state of government and morals in the country. A flood of letters arrived at the Hermitage begging him to seek the presidency. He began to reconsider.

In 1822 the Tennessee legislature nominated Andrew Jackson to run for president in the upcoming 1824 election. They also named him as a candidate for the U.S. Senate, in case he didn't win the presidential race, and he was elected to

the Senate in 1823. Leaving Rachel and the Hermitage once more, Jackson went to Washington to represent Tennessee. He worked hard to fulfill his duties. Since his first time in the Senate more than twenty years earlier, Jackson had learned to control his

✧ ——————————————

When Jackson became a senator in 1823, he was a distinguished country gentleman. This portrait shows his Hermitage estate in the background.

temper and to behave with dignity. "When it becomes necessary to . . . be meek," he wrote, "no man can command his temper better than I."

A CORRUPT BARGAIN

The 1824 presidential election campaign was already in progress when Jackson arrived in the Senate. The three candidates besides Andrew Jackson were Henry Clay, John Quincy Adams, and William Crawford. None of these men was as popular as the hero of New Orleans. Jackson pledged to end corruption and to reform the government. When the election was held, Jackson received 155,800 votes, compared to 104,300 for Adams. The other candidates were far behind. Although Jackson had the most votes, U.S. presidents are not elected by popular vote alone. Presidents must also be voted in by a group of electors, called the electoral college, that is chosen to vote on behalf of each state. Here, too, Jackson was ahead, with 99 electoral votes over 84 for Adams.

Jackson ran against Henry Clay, John Quincy Adams, and William Crawford (left to right) *in the presidential election of 1824.*

It was still not enough. Although he had the most electoral votes, it was not a majority of the total of 261 electoral votes. To become president, Jackson needed 131 electoral votes. Without this majority, the Constitution required the House of Representatives to make the final decision. As the vote went to the House, the corruption that Jackson was trying to fight took a hand in the election's outcome. Henry Clay was out of the running for president, but it was alleged that he had been promised an important post in John Quincy Adams's administration. As Speaker of the House of Representatives, Clay used his influence to sway the vote. Adams was elected president.

Jackson and his supporters were stunned. They felt that the election had been stolen, and they called it a "corrupt bargain." "I weep for the Liberty of my country," said Jackson. The "rights of the people have been bartered for promises of office."

A wave of anger swept through the country, especially among the common people who had supported Jackson. They felt as though their votes did not count. They hoped to make things right four years later. As reluctant as he had been to enter the race, Jackson looked forward to the next presidential election. This time he was determined to win.

Jackson and his followers began their campaign soon after Adams took office. They opposed Adams in all he tried to do. New supporters gathered behind Jackson, including Martin Van Buren of New York and even Adams's vice president, John C. Calhoun. After the controversy of the 1824 election, Andrew Jackson and these supporters did not feel comfortable being in the same political party as their foes. They formed a new party that came to be called the Democratic Party.

The presidential campaign of 1828 was a long, hard fight. Jackson and the Democrats promised to stand up for the interests of the common people. John Quincy Adams's supporters, who had nominated him for a second term, tried to destroy Jackson's reputation by hurling accusations at him. Adams's supporters brought up Jackson's gambling as a young man and his duel with Dickinson. They even criticized the military career of which Old Hickory was so proud. But worst of all were the old accusations about his

This handbill, published during the campaign, condemned Jackson for ordering the execution of six soldiers charged with desertion and mutiny during the Creek War.

marriage to Rachel. The Cincinnati *Gazette* wrote, "Gen. Jackson prevailed upon the wife of Lewis Roberts [Robards] . . . to desert her husband." In Washington society, unkind things were said about Rachel's appearance and her country ways.

Jackson was able to deal with all these charges—except the ones concerning Rachel. It pained him to see how hurt she was. She had never enjoyed the public spotlight, and her health began to deteriorate under the torrent of ugly words. Jackson was furious and campaigned with more determination than ever. His own supporters were not above a bit of mudslinging, reminding the public of the bargain made by Adams and Clay and stirring up other scandals.

Jackson also renewed his pledge to end corruption and to represent the needs of common folks. The American people responded to his call for reform. He won the election of 1828 by a clear majority of both popular and electoral votes, with John C. Calhoun as vice president.

HEARTBREAK

Old Hickory had become the people's president, but it was at a terrible cost. Devastated by the brutality of the campaign, Rachel fell ill. "Her energy subsided, her spirits drooped, and her health declined—She has been heard to speak but seldom," said a friend. After the election, Rachel dreaded being in the public eye as the president's wife, and her condition grew even worse. On December 17, she suffered a heart attack. Jackson stayed at her side constantly, comforting and caring for her. A few days later, she had another heart attack. "I am fainting!" she cried out, and died.

*From the time of Rachel's death until the end of his life, Jackson
wore this tiny portrait of her on a cord around his neck.*

——————————— ✧ ———————————

Jackson would not accept that his beloved wife of thir-
ty-eight years was gone. He sat by her bed for hours, refus-
ing food or drink, hoping that somehow she might be
revived. When he finally was able to accept the truth, he
blamed his enemies for her death. "She was murdered," he
cried, "murdered by slanders that pierced her heart! May
God Almighty forgive her murderers as I know she forgave
them. I never can!"

On Christmas Eve, 1828, Rachel Jackson was buried in
the garden at the Hermitage. Jackson's heart was broken.

CHAPTER EIGHT

THE PEOPLE'S PRESIDENT

*"It was a proud day for the people. General
Jackson is their own President."*
—the newspaper *Argus of Western America*

Andrew Jackson was inaugurated as the seventh president
of the United States on March 4, 1829. It was a clear,
sunny day. Thousands of people had streamed into
Washington for the occasion.

Most of the presidents before Jackson had been edu-
cated and wealthy. Now the common people of America
had come to see their own president take office. Jackson's
plain-speaking ways appealed to small-town folk and to
those from the frontier. Crowds from around the country
gathered near the Capitol to watch the ceremony.

Jackson was dressed in black, still mourning deeply for
Rachel. At sixty-one years old, he was tall and lean, with a
long, craggy face. His thick hair had become completely
white. He mounted the steps of the Capitol to take the

In his inaugural address, President Jackson (left) promised "the zealous dedication of [his] humble abilities to [the people's] service and their good."

———————————————— ✧ ————————————————

oath of office. His speech was short and to the point. He emphasized his view that the purpose of government was to protect the rights and liberty of the people. He promised to cut down on spending and to pay off the national debt.

Not everyone was happy that Jackson had won. His opponents were critical of the noisy, excited crowd of admirers and onlookers. "The reign of KING MOB seemed triumphant," one of them remarked.

President Jackson ignored the skeptics and took charge. His first task was to appoint a presidential cabinet made up of the heads of government departments. One of Jackson's most trusted advisers was the brilliant Martin Van Buren, whom he chose as secretary of state. A president usually meets with his full cabinet, but Jackson preferred to consult with a small group of loyal friends who became known as the "kitchen cabinet." The president listened to these unofficial advisers, but even their influence was small. Andrew Jackson made his own decisions.

One of his early decisions was to call for appointed government officials to resign from office with the begin-

Martin Van Buren

ning of a new administration. He felt that public service should only last for a short time and that keeping officials in their jobs over several terms led to dishonesty and corruption. Jackson believed that these positions should be filled by each new president. This practice, which came to be known as the "spoils system," was widely criticized.

During his campaign, Andrew had pledged to pay off the national debt by reducing corruption and adjusting the government's budget. He followed through on his promise emphasizing this measure in his first message to Congress. Despite some opposition from officials who had to change their habits, the national debt was reduced considerably after only one year.

THE INDIAN REMOVAL ACT

Early in his presidency, Jackson had to face the difficult "Indian question." The question was how to gain control over Native American territory to make room for white farmers and businesspeople. Jackson still believed that the destiny of the country was tied to expansion, and there was no place for Native Americans in his vision of America.

President Jackson's solution was simple but harsh. He proposed that all Native Americans who lived east of the Mississippi River be "removed," or resettled west of the Mississippi. In 1830 Congress passed the Indian Removal Act. This law authorized the government to make treaties with the Indians, granting them land in the West in exchange for their ancestral lands. Native Americans, including the Choctaw,

————————— ✧ —————————

When calling for the Indian Removal Act, Jackson stated that the "emigration should be voluntary." Nevertheless, thousands of Native Americans made the hard journey westward against their will.

Chickasaw, Creek, and Seminole tribes, were forced out of their homes in Georgia, Mississippi, Alabama, Illinois, and Florida. The entire Cherokee nation was sent on a long and difficult march westward. Some estimates say that as many as four thousand Cherokees died along the way. Their forced migration became known as the Trail of Tears.

STATES' RIGHTS

Another problem facing Jackson involved the rights of the states versus the power of the national government. The debate had been going on for years. Jackson supported the idea that people should have power over local issues. But some states wanted to go further. They wanted to nullify, or refuse to recognize and obey, national laws with which they disagreed. One of these laws was a tariff bill that Congress had passed in 1828. This law put a tax on goods coming into the United States from abroad. Southerners objected because they traded cotton for these imported products. They worried that the extra tax would hurt them financially. Vice President John C. Calhoun, who was from South Carolina, also protested the tariff bill. He claimed that the country was a loose union of states, and that a state should have the right to nullify a federal law, or even to secede (or withdraw) from the Union. Senator Daniel Webster of Massachusetts pointed out that the national government represented the will of all the people. "Liberty *and* Union," he proclaimed, "now and forever, one and inseparable."

Andrew Jackson was a Southerner who generally supported the rights of states, and the advocates of nullification assumed that he sided with them. The opposite was true. Jackson believed that the future of the nation depended on

In 1831 disagreements and scandal caused many members of Jackson's administration to resign. This popular cartoon shows Jackson being abandoned by his advisers and cabinet members.

✧ ————————————————

a strong Union. The existence of the country would be in danger if every state could secede on a whim.

The president made his own view clear at a dinner party in Washington, D.C., in 1830. Calhoun and other Southerners had openly declared their support for states' rights. Then the president stood up and raised his glass. "Our Union," he toasted, "it must be preserved." His statement was met with dead silence. The Southerners now knew exactly where Jackson stood.

The crisis built as South Carolina continued to consider withdrawing from the Union. Jackson took strong measures against the supporters of nullification. In December 1832, he sent a proclamation directly to the people of South Carolina, promoting the strength of the Union and warning that nullification would destroy the nation. In 1833 he signed a new tariff bill that lowered the tax, but he also made it clear that he would not hesitate to use force to prevent the state from seceding. South Carolina and the nullifiers finally backed down. Jackson had held the Union together against the worst internal threat it had ever faced.

POLITICS AND PETTICOATS

From the beginning of his presidency, Andrew Jackson met with frustrating opposition. An early problem, nicknamed the "petticoat affair," tested his loyalty to friends.

John Eaton, the secretary of war, had served as Jackson's aide and associate for a long time, and they were close friends. Jackson described the young man as "more like a son to me than anything else." Eaton's wife, Peggy, was said to have been wild and flirtatious before her marriage. The wives of other cabinet members gossiped about Peggy and refused to accept her into their friendship or society. But Jackson treated Peggy with kindness and consideration. He remembered how deeply rumors had hurt Rachel, and he firmly defended Peggy. "I would resign the Presidency sooner than desert my friend Eaton," he declared.

Rumors continued to swirl around Peggy Eaton. Each time she was attacked or excluded from social affairs, Jackson steadfastly stood behind her. Soon the controversy over Peggy Eaton extended into national politics. Disagreements flared among the members of the cabinet, interfering with vital business. Jackson angrily blamed Vice President John C. Calhoun for causing much of the trouble and lost confidence in him. Jackson and Calhoun never saw eye-to-eye again, and Calhoun eventually resigned from his position as vice president.

Despite Jackson's determination to do what he felt was right, it was clear that the controversy in the cabinet was taking time away from his duties as president. The matter was finally settled when John Eaton and many of the other cabinet members resigned from their positions (see cartoon, facing page). Jackson was sorry to see Eaton leave, but with his absence the commotion over Peggy came to an end, and President Jackson was able to devote his time to more important matters.

Still, he feared that his victory was only temporary. He believed that the nullifiers in the southern states would one day "blow up a storm." "These men," he warned, "would do any act to destroy this union and form a southern confederacy."

INTERNATIONAL RELATIONS

Jackson was as forceful in the way he conducted foreign affairs as he was in domestic business. He told Congress that his policy was "to ask nothing that is not clearly right, and to submit to nothing that is wrong." He sent a firm message to foreign countries that the United States of America was a free and independent nation and should be treated with respect. His strong stand helped to end some British restrictions on U.S. trade and to recover money that foreign countries owed to the United States. He was the first president to negotiate commercial treaties with Asian countries such as Japan and the nations that would become

Vietnam and Thailand. He also established diplomatic relations with Russia, Denmark, Portugal, Turkey, Morocco, Mexico, and Chile.

At the end of his first term, Jackson was as popular as ever. One newspaper wrote, "The devotion to him is altogether personal, without reference to his course of policy." Even citizens who disagreed with some of his beliefs voted for him. Andrew Jackson was overwhelmingly reelected in 1832.

THE BANK

During Jackson's second term, he accomplished his goal of paying off the entire national debt. He also fought one of the fiercest battles of his presidency.

The Bank of the United States had been established by Alexander Hamilton when the nation was founded. The new, small country had needed a stable financial institution to survive. By the time Jackson became president, economic conditions had changed, and Jackson believed that the powerful Bank of the United States had grown too large and corrupt. He accused it of strangling the common people and small-business owners. He wanted to change the system so that small banks across the country would be able to compete.

Congress disagreed. The bank's charter, giving it permission to continue operating, was due to expire in 1836. In 1832 the Senate voted to approve a new charter for the Bank of the United States.

Jackson was furious. He called the bank a monster and claimed that it was trying to kill him. *But I will kill it!* he vowed. When the Senate's bill arrived at his desk in July 1832, he vetoed the measure, saying, "when the laws

This political cartoon shows the columns of the Bank of the United States crashing to the ground as Jackson finally triumphs.

—————————————— ✧ ——————————————

undertake . . . to make the rich richer . . . the humble members of society . . . have a right to complain of the injustice of their Government." Congress tried to override this veto but failed. Jackson followed up his veto with a bill that stopped the deposit of government money into the bank. He also began to propose alternative ways to distribute this money and to spread business to smaller banks. These actions weakened the Bank of the United States, but in 1834 another bill to renew the bank's charter went to Congress. When this bill failed to pass, the bank finally collapsed.

TEXAS

Near the end of Jackson's term, he turned his attention to a new frontier to the west. The territory of Texas belonged to Mexico when Jackson was president. Jackson wanted to add

Texas to the United States. He tried to persuade Mexico to sell the territory, but his attempts failed. Sam Houston, who had served as a general in the U.S. Army and was an old friend of Jackson's, also wanted to win Texas for the United States. In 1836 Houston led an army of Texans into combat against Mexican forces. Houston and his troops won the territory's independence, and Texas eventually became a state of the Union.

THE OLD SOLDIER

During his years as president, Andrew Jackson projected a public image of boldness, strength, and action. It probably would have surprised most people to know that his health was poor. He often coughed up blood, and he was in con-stant agony from his old wounds. Doctors believed that bleeding could relieve pain, and Jackson sometimes bled himself by opening a vein with a penknife. He spent long hours working on matters of state, but there were times when he was so ill and weak that he had to do these duties in bed or on a couch.

---✧

Jackson's stately pose in this portrait by Ralph E. W. Earl gives no hint of his failing health.

Somehow Jackson found the will to overcome his physical weaknesses. He stayed true to his belief that the government belonged to the people, and the President's House was always open to visitors from all walks of life. He received everyone with great friendliness, and his charm, honesty, and intelligence impressed most of them.

Jackson still had enemies, but even death threats did not bother him. "I try to live my life," he asserted, "as if death might come at any moment." That moment almost came in 1835, when a gunman attempted to murder the

—————————————— ✧ ——————————————

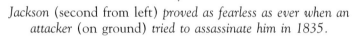

Jackson (second from left) proved as fearless as ever when an attacker *(on ground)* tried to assassinate him in 1835.

president. When the attacker's gun misfired, sixty-seven-year-old Jackson started to rush at him himself before bystanders seized the man and threw him to the ground. It was the first assassination attempt against a president of the United States.

This incident only served to deepen the public's love and respect for Jackson. His firm convictions and strong personality made him the most forceful president who had yet occupied the position. He knew what he wanted to accomplish, and he usually managed to achieve his goals. He refused to give in to Congress, and he used the veto power more than any president had before. Jackson transformed the presidency into the strongest branch of the U.S. government, decreasing the power of the legislature. His enemies accused him of being a tyrant and called him King Andrew. He responded that it was the duty of a president to represent and carry out "the sacred trust" of the people.

When it came time for Andrew Jackson to leave

———————————— ✧
One political cartoonist depicted President Jackson as a king determined to rule without regard for democracy or the Constitution.

office in 1837, the old soldier was the most popular U.S. president since George Washington. Throngs lined the streets near the railway station to cheer him as he boarded the train that would take him home to Tennessee. Thousands of people greeted him at stops along the way, and one newspaper reported that the crowds had come to see "the greatest man of the age." At one stop, as a crowd watched the president's train disappear into the distance, an onlooker remarked that it was "as if a bright star had gone out of the sky."

CHAPTER NINE

LAST YEARS AT THE HERMITAGE

*"My son, try to remember that you have looked
on the face of Andrew Jackson."*
—Sam Houston

Jackson was looking forward to a quiet retirement at his beloved Hermitage. His adopted son Andrew Jackson Jr. had been running the plantation in Jackson's absence. But Andrew Jr. wasn't as skilled as Rachel had been. In fact, he had done a terrible job. He drank heavily and spent too much money. By the time his father returned, Andrew Jr. had run up enormous debts.

Jackson promptly took control of business dealings himself. He set to work putting the Hermitage's affairs in order, and he eventually paid off all the debts that Andrew Jr. had incurred. Again and again, the younger Jackson got into debt. Each time, his father rescued him. Jackson loved his adopted son and never blamed him for the trouble that he caused.

The old soldier's health got worse each year. In addition to constant pain and weakness, he lost his vision in one eye and could barely hear. He suffered from terrible headaches, and he had difficulty breathing.

Despite his ailments, Jackson stayed as active as he could. He read newspapers and was keenly interested in what was going on in the country. Friends and politicians came calling at the Hermitage. The house was also filled with the nephews and nieces to whom he and Rachel had given a home. Now, their own children accompanied them. Jackson loved seeing them, and he tried to hide his suffering.

But Jackson's friends couldn't help noticing that his condition was worsening. By 1845 illness had caused his body

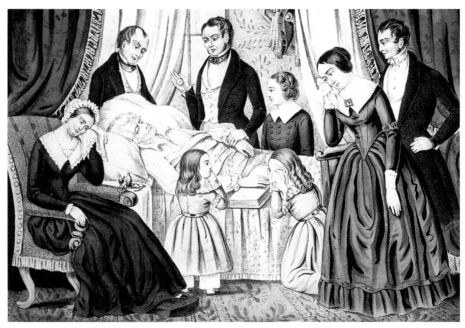

Mourners gather around Jackson's deathbed.

to swell. He looked so bad that one visitor remarked, "If it were any other man, I could scarcely suppose he would live a week." Jackson, too, knew that death was near, but he remained alert and clearheaded until the end. He said that he wished "to be buried without display or pomp." When those who were gathered around him wept, he soothed them. "Do not cry. Be good children, and we shall all meet in Heaven."

On June 8, 1845, Andrew Jackson died at the age of seventy-eight. He was buried at the Hermitage beside his beloved Rachel.

THE AGE OF JACKSON

Not every president has a historical period named after him. There is no Age of Washington or Age of Jefferson. But the years of Andrew Jackson's presidency, and even beyond, are called the Age of Jackson.

There are several reasons for this label. One actually has little to do with Jackson. Important changes in the United States during Jackson's lifetime made it a memorable age in many ways. Westward expansion was stretching the boundaries of the United States. More uses were being found for natural resources such as coal and water. New inventions, including Eli Whitney's cotton gin, McCormick's mechanical reaper, the Colt revolver, and Samuel Morse's telegraph, increased efficiency and communication in the young nation. Transportation sped up as roads, railroads, and canals crisscrossed the land.

Andrew Jackson himself brought an uncommon forcefulness to the presidency. When he was dying, one of his servants remarked, "If [General Jackson] wants to go to Heaven who's to stop him?" This will and determination was the basis of Andrew Jackson's success throughout his life. Before he became president, it marked his career as a lawyer and judge. It showed in the dedication that earned him the nickname of Old Hickory, and it helped him achieve victory at New Orleans. His humble beginnings on the frontier made him tough but also gave him a sense of compassion. He was determined to make his nation a true democracy that belonged to the people. Jackson changed the presidency—and the country—permanently.

Jackson also brought something else new to the presidency—a fervent belief that government must represent more people than just the wealthy and the privileged few. The

Jackson was tough and determined all his life.

✧

programs he fought for were based on this belief. People still refer to Jacksonian Democracy. In Jackson's time, that meant supporting the interests of farmers and small-business owners, laborers, and struggling pioneers. Modern Jacksonian Democrats want the government to help improve the lives of working people, immigrants, and the underprivileged. As the people's president, Andrew Jackson helped to establish a new type of democracy that lasted well beyond his age.

TIMELINE

1767   Andrew Jackson is born in the Carolina Waxhaws.

1780–1781   Hugh Jackson dies in Charleston, South Carolina. Andrew and Robert are captured by British troops. Robert dies of smallpox.

1781   Jackson's mother, Elizabeth Hutchinson Jackson, dies of cholera.

1783–1784   Jackson teaches school in the Waxhaws. Jackson moves to Salisbury, North Carolina, to study law.

1787   Jackson earns his license as an attorney and practices law in North Carolina.

1788   Jackson is appointed public prosecutor in the Western District of North Carolina and travels to Nashville.

1791   Jackson marries Rachel Donelson Robards.

1794   Jackson remarries Rachel for legal reasons.

1796   Jackson is elected as a Tennessee representative to the U.S. House of Representatives.

1797   Jackson is elected as a U.S. senator from Tennessee.

1798   Jackson is elected as a judge of the Superior Court of Tennessee.

1802   Jackson is elected major general of the Tennessee militia.

1804   Jackson and Rachel purchase the Hermitage.

1806   Jackson kills Charles Dickinson in a duel and is severely wounded himself.

1809   Jackson and Rachel adopt Andrew Jackson Jr.

1812   The War of 1812 begins.

1813   Jackson leads troops to Natchez, Mississippi, and is nicknamed Old Hickory by his men.

1814   Jackson's troops defeat the Creek Indians in the Creek War.

1815   Jackson's troops defeat the British at the Battle of New Orleans.

1817–1818   Jackson leads troops against the Seminoles and invades Spanish Florida.

1821   Jackson is appointed governor of Florida Territory.

1823   Jackson is elected as a U.S. senator from Tennessee.

1824   Jackson receives the most popular and electoral votes in the presidential election.

1825   The election goes to the House of Representatives and Jackson loses to John Quincy Adams.

1828   Jackson is elected president. Rachel dies at the Hermitage. The tariff and nullification crisis begins.

1830   Jackson signs the Indian Removal Act.

1832   Jackson is reelected president and the Bank of the United States crisis begins.

1835   The national debt is paid. Jackson escapes the first assassination attempt on a U.S. president.

1837   Jackson leaves Washington, D.C., for the Hermitage.

1845   Jackson dies at the Hermitage and is buried next to Rachel.

SOURCE NOTES

7 "First Inaugural Address of Andrew Jackson," *The Avalon Project at Yale Law School,* 1996, <http://www.yale.edu /lawweb/avalon/presiden /inaug/jackson1.htm> (December 11, 2001).

9 James Parton, *Life of Andrew Jackson in Three Volumes* (New York: Mason Brothers, 1860), 1:64.

15 *World Book Encyclopedia,* vol. 5, S. V. "Declaration of Independence."

15 Ibid.

17 Marquis James, *The Life of Andrew Jackson, Complete in One Volume* (New York: Bobbs-Merrill Company, 1938), 18.

17 Ibid., 17.

20–21 Ibid., 20.

21 Ibid., 22.

23 Burke Davis, *Old Hickory: A Life of Andrew Jackson* (New York: Dial Press, 1977), 6.

24 James, *Life of Andrew Jackson,* 28.

24 Ibid., 29.

25 Ibid., 35.

27 Robert V. Remini, *The Life of Andrew Jackson* (New York: Harper & Row, 1988), 7.

29 Ibid., 10.

29 James, *Life of Andrew Jackson,* 35.

29 Ibid., 37.

31–32 Remini, *Life of Andrew Jackson,* 14–15.

35 Robert V. Remini, *Andrew Jackson* (New York: Twayne Publishers, 1966), 51.

36 James, *Life of Andrew Jackson,* 52.

36 Ibid., 53.

38 Remini, *Life of Andrew Jackson,* 19.

41 Ibid., 35.

42 James, *Life of Andrew Jackson,* 80.

42 Ibid., 82.

42 Remini, *Life of Andrew Jackson,* 40.

43 James, *Life of Andrew Jackson,* 89.

43 Remini, *Life of Andrew Jackson,* 43.

43 Ibid.

43–44 Ibid., 44.

45 Ibid., 46.

45 Ibid.

45 Ibid.

46 James, *Life of Andrew Jackson,* 93.

47 Parton, *Life of Andrew Jackson,* 1:249.

47 Remini, *Life of Andrew Jackson,* 49.

49 James, *Life of Andrew Jackson,* 113.

50 The Ladies' Hermitage Association, *The Hermitage, Home of President Andrew Jackson* (Hermitage, TN: The Ladies' Hermitage Association, 1997), n.p.

51 James, *Life of Andrew Jackson.,* 115.

51 Ibid., 118.

51 Ibid.

51 Ibid.

52 Ibid.

54 Parton, *Life of Andrew Jackson,* 1:435.

56 James, *Life of Andrew Jackson,* 141.

56–57 Ibid., 144.

57 Ibid., 147.

57 Remini, *Life of Andrew Jackson,* 63.

58 James, *Life of Andrew Jackson,* 149.
59 Remini, *Life of Andrew Jackson,* 67.
60 Ibid., 70.
61 Ibid., 72.
64 James, *Life of Andrew Jackson,* 201.
65 Remini, *Life of Andrew Jackson,* 90.
65 Ibid., 91.
65 Ibid.
66 Ibid., 95.
67 Ibid., 99.
67 Ibid.
68 Ibid., 108.
68 Davis, *Old Hickory,* 149.
68 Remini, *Life of Andrew Jackson,* 109.
68 Ibid., 110.
68 Ibid.
68–69 Ibid., 111.
70 Ibid., 73.
72 Ibid., 118.
74 Ibid., 128.
74 Ibid., 124.
75 Ibid., 145.
77 Ibid., 134.
79 James, *Life of Andrew Jackson,* 330.
80 Robert V. Remini, *Andrew Jackson and the Course of American Freedom, 1822–1832* (New York: Harper & Row, 1981), 59.
81 Remini, *Life of Andrew Jackson,* 155.
81 Ibid.
83 Ibid., 163.
83 Ibid., 474.
83 Ibid., 479.
84 Davis, *Old Hickory,* 230.
85 Remini, *Life of Andrew Jackson,* 181.
86 "First Inaugural Address," *Avalon Project.*
86 Remini, *Life of Andrew Jackson,* 180.

88 Anthony F. C. Wallace, *The Long, Bitter Trail: Andrew Jackson and the Indians* (New York: Hill and Wang, 1993), 124.
89 James, *Life of Andrew Jackson,* 531.
90 Ibid., 539.
91 Remini, *Life of Andrew Jackson,* 173.
91 Davis, *Old Hickory,* 290.
92 "President Jackson's Proclamation Regarding Nullification, December 10, 1832," *The Avalon Project at Yale Law School,* 1996, <http://www.yale.edu/lawweb/avalon/presiden/proclamations/jack01.htm> (April 18, 2002).
92 James, *Life of Andrew Jackson,* 622.
92 Remini, *Life of Andrew Jackson,* 283.
93 Ibid., 237.
93 Ibid., 227.
93–94 Ibid., 229.
96 Davis, *Old Hickory,* 345.
97 Robert V. Remini, *The Revolutionary Age of Andrew Jackson* (New York: Harper & Row, 1976), 160.
97 Remini, *Andrew Jackson,* 164.
98 Remini, *Life of Andrew Jackson,* 336.
98 James, *Life of Andrew Jackson,* 724.
99 Ibid., 786.
101 Remini, *Life of Andrew Jackson,* 355.
101 James, *Life of Andrew Jackson,* 783.
101 Ibid., 785.
102 Remini, *Revolutionary Age of Andrew Jackson,* 184.

BIBLIOGRAPHY

Andrist, Ralph K. *Andrew Jackson, Soldier and Statesman.* New York: American Heritage Publishing Co., 1963.

Coke, Fletch. *Jackson's Hermitage.* Hermitage, TN: The Ladies' Hermitage Association, 1979.

Curtis, James C. *Andrew Jackson and the Search for Vindication.* Boston: Little, Brown, 1976.

Davis, Burke. *Old Hickory: A Life of Andrew Jackson.* New York: Dial Press, 1977.

De Kay, Ormonde, Jr. *Meet Andrew Jackson.* New York: Random House, 1967.

James, Marquis. *The Life of Andrew Jackson, Complete in One Volume.* New York: Bobbs-Merrill Company, 1938.

Judson, Karen. *Andrew Jackson.* Berkeley Heights, NJ: Enslow, 1997.

Ladies' Hermitage Association, The. *The Hermitage, Home of President Andrew Jackson.* Hermitage, TN: The Ladies' Hermitage Association, 1997.

Meltzer, Milton. *Andrew Jackson and His America.* New York: Franklin Watts, 1993.

Parton, James. *Life of Andrew Jackson in Three Volumes.* New York: Mason Brothers, 1860.

Potts, Steve. *Andrew Jackson: A Photo-Illustrated Biography.* Mankato, MN: Bridgestone Books, 1996.

Remini, Robert V. *Andrew Jackson.* New York: Twayne Publishers, 1966.

———. *Andrew Jackson and the Course of American Freedom, 1822–1832.* New York: Harper and Row, 1981.

———. *The Life of Andrew Jackson.* New York: Harper & Row, 1988.

———. *The Revolutionary Age of Andrew Jackson.* New York: Harper & Row, 1976.

Schlesinger, Arthur M., Jr. *The Age of Jackson*. Boston: Little, Brown, 1946.

Van Deusen, Glyndon G. *The Jacksonian Era, 1828–1848*. New York: Harper and Row, 1959.

FURTHER READING

Bealer, Alex W. *Only the Names Remain: The Cherokees and the Trail of Tears*. Boston: Little, Brown, 1996.

Collier, Christopher. *Andrew Jackson's America, 1824–1850*. New York: Benchmark Books, 1999.

Dolan, Edward F. *The American Revolution: How We Fought the War of Independence*. Brookfield, CT: Millbrook Press, 1995.

Gaines, Ann. *Andrew Jackson: Our Seventh President*. Chanhassen, MN: Child's World, 2002.

Greenblatt, Miriam. *The War of 1812*. New York: Facts On File, 1994.

Hoig, Stan. *Night of the Cruel Moon: Cherokee Removal and the Trail of Tears*. New York: Facts on File, 1996.

King, David C. *New Orleans*. New York: Twenty-First Century Books, 1998.

Miller, Brandon Marie. *Growing Up in Revolution and the New Nation: 1775 to 1800*. Minneapolis: Lerner Publications, 2003.

Osinski, Alice. *Andrew Jackson*. Chicago: Children's Press, 1987.

Parlin, John. *Andrew Jackson: Pioneer and President*. New York: Chelsea Juniors, 1991.

Weber, Michael. *The Young Republic*. Austin, TX: Raintree Steck-Vaughn, 2000.

Whitelaw, Nancy. *Andrew Jackson: Frontier President*. Greensboro, NC: Morgan Reynolds, 2001.

INDEX

ABOUT THE AUTHOR

Carol H. Behrman was born in Brooklyn, New York. She graduated from City College of New York and attended Columbia University's Teachers' College, where she majored in education. She married Edward Behrman, an accountant, and moved to Fair Lawn, New Jersey, where they raised three children. They currently reside in Sarasota, Florida.

For many years, Behrman taught grades five through eight at the Glen Ridge Middle School in New Jersey. She has written twenty books, fiction and nonfiction, for children and young adults, as well as five writing textbooks. Her previous biographies include *Fiddler to the World: The Inspiring Life of Itzhak Perlman, Roberto Clemente,* and *Miss Dr. Lucy,* the story of the first woman dentist in America.

✧

PHOTO ACKNOWLEDGMENTS

The images in this book are used with the permission of: The White House, pp. 1, 7, 9, 15, 25, 35, 47, 54, 75, 85, 99; Independence National Historical Park, p. 2; Library of Congress, pp. 6 (LC-USZ62-1805), 19 (LC-USZ62-103793), 24 (LC (USZ62-5852), 26 (LC-USZC2-2131), 33 (LC-USZ62-02630), 44 (LC0USZ62-60870), 59, 86 (LC-USZC4-7731), 90 (LC-USZ2-92280), 94 (LC-USZ62-809), 103; Tennessee State Museum Photographic Archives, pp. 10, 80 (right); North Wind Pictures, pp. 13, 14, 16, 20, 52, 63, 66, 71, 73, 80 (center), 96; The Hermitage, pp. 21, 22, 38, 48, 76, 79, 84, 95, 100 (photo by Dennis Darling); © NC Museum of History, p. 31; Provided by Nashville Public Television from the Court of Quarter Session book 1792-96, p. 105, p. 37; Brown Brothers, pp. 40, 55, 56, 80 (left); Art Archive/Museé du Château de Versailles/Dagli Orti, p. 41; Tennessee State Museum, Tennessee Historical Society Collection pp. 45, 87; National Museum of American History, Smithsonian Institution, pp. 46, 92 (DeWitt Collection); Tennessee State Library & Archives, Tennessee Historical Society Collection, pp. 50, 97; Museums of the City of Mobile, AL, p. 61; New York Public Library; Special Collections, p. 62; © CORBIS, p. 72; Florida State Archives, p. 77; Historic New Orleans Collection, p. 82; Woolaroc Museum, Bartlesville, OK, p. 88.

Front cover: courtesy of the Library of Congress.